To Lucille,
Expect the Best!

DISTINCTIVE *Homes* OF AMERICA

VOLUME III
NAPLES
FLORIDA

BY GLENN D. HETTINGER, AIA, ICAA

DISTINCTIVE Homes OF AMERICA™

CREDITS

PUBLISHED BY

GDH Architects, P.A.

dba DISTINCTIVE HOMES OF AMERICA

38 Valencia Street, Suite 200, Ponte Vedra Beach, FL 32082

904.881.8100

www.DistinctiveHomesOfAmerica.com

GLENN D. HETTINGER, AIA, ICAA

Author / Principal Photographer / Managing Editor

Concept & Project Direction

DIANE ZWACK

Creative Director / Graphic Artist

14 CONTRIBUTING PHOTOGRAPHERS

Lori Hamilton Photography, Giovanni Photography (John Sciarrino),
Naples Kenny (Ken Siebenhar), Keith Isaac Photography, CJ Walker Photography, Inc., Craig Hildebrand Photography, Dana Hoff Photography, Jim Freeman Photography, Sargent Architectural Photography,
Tom Harper Photography, Windham Studio, Inc. (Aaron Denton), Dave Ross Photography
Randall Perry Photography & Doug Thompson Photography

CONTRIBUTING WRITERS

Many Homeowners, Architects, Interior Designers and General Contractors of the 50 featured homes gave insight into the distinctiveness of their design and building projects. They are quoted in the home layouts in and around the pictures of their impressive work.

All rights reserved. No portion of this book may be reproduced — mechanically, electronically, or by any other means including photocopying — without written permission from the publisher, except for brief passages that may be quoted for reviews.

Copyright © 2014 Glenn D. Hettinger

First Edition

ISBN-13: 978-0-9908567-0-2 / ISBN-10: 0990856704

Printed in Hong Kong, China by Crash Pape

First Printing: December 2014

10 9 8 7 6 5 4 3 2 1

JACKET/ COVER DESIGN: The seven homes featured span the diverse spectrum of architectural design that makes Naples a one-of-a-kind community,
and represents the unique people that make it their home.

FRONT COVER: Photos by Glenn Hettinger

BACK COVER: Photos by Naples Kenny, CJ Walker & Glenn Hettinger

DUST JACKET FLAPS: Photos by Glenn Hettinger

TITLE PAGE ONE: Photo by Lori Hamilton

224 pages, with more than 700 full-color pictures.

visit **www.DistinctiveHomesOfAmerica.com** for further information.

BOOK ENDORSEMENTS

"Your books on Distinctive Homes are amazing peeks into homes most of us will only admire from the curb. Thanks for taking us inside some of the most distinctive homes in the country." Be On-Purpose!
— Kevin W. McCarthy, *CEO, On-Purpose Business Advisors*

"Congrats, your books are not only coffee table quality, but a valued reference in our office when researching authentic design detailing for residential design. Keep it up we are big fans!"
— Ken Puncerelli, *CEO, LAI Design Group*

"I seldom pay full price for a book or read them cover to cover. But I'm glad that I did both things with your book. That has LONG been one of my favorite areas and it was fascinating to read the details and backstories behind some of the newer homes. And your photography was spectacular."
— ScottAllen Barber – *Kenilworth, IL*

"I was given your book as a gift two years ago and I still love to study its pages. The homes are outstanding and the architecture for this area is truly distinctive. I would recommend this book to anyone who loves looking at beautiful homes and decorating!"
— Christina Schneider, *Realtor*

"I have just finished going through your past two books and feel compelled to write and congratulate you on the most detail photographed presentation of large home displays that I've ever seen. Your apparent personal relationship with the owners made your coverage that much more interesting. You captured perfectly the most magnificent homes. I can tell you will be finishing more books in your series of homes around the US so please leave me on your mailing list. I want to have every one of them in my collection! You are doing a beautiful job of capturing these impressive homes for future reference."
— Jack Bertoglio, *Developer*

© Craig Hildebrand

ACKNOWLEDGMENTS

"IF YOU'RE LUCKY ENOUGH TO LIVE IN NAPLES YOU'RE LUCKY ENOUGH"

Anyone who has lived or vacationed around Naples, Florida has been blessed. That is why I hope that what is shared in this book will be a blessing to all who read it. I have to first thank all of the homeowners who graciously shared their distinctive homes in this way. I had to take these pictures when the sun and clouds were just right and usually on short notice. I so appreciate the cooperation and hospitality that the fifty distinctive homeowners have granted me.

Special recognition goes to all of the architects, home designers, interior designers, builders, craftsmen, Realtors and other professionals for their distinctive creations. I seek their forgiveness for hounding them for quotes, photographs and other information about the homes on which they worked. That goes especially to Jenny Rogers Haire and Barbie Rogers Kellam for all of their help in this area. It is my hope that all will benefit from this additional exposure of their outstanding creations.

Thanks go to the many contributing photographers, both amateur and professional. The book is so much better due to their contributions. I must especially single out the fabulous photographs from Lori Hamilton Photography, Giovanni Photography (John Sciarrino), CJ Walker Photography, Inc., Keith Isaac Photography, and Naples Kenny (Ken Siebenhar). They all lent their terrific images on multiple homes.

As you look through the book you will be treated to the tremendous design and layout work of our graphic artist Diane Zwack. Her design talents and knowledge of publishing made the book possible.

My appreciation goes to my life-long friend Terry Tait and his wife Nancy and my cousin Anita Chaney and her husband Bob for their joyful hospitality in housing me in Naples. I thank Mathew Kragh for lending me his boat. That enabled me to select the homes and to take my many waterside pictures.

And most of all, I am so blessed to have the support of my wonderful wife Jean, our four fantastic sons Sam, Ben, Greg & Alex, and four fabulous daughters-in-law Laura, Jenny, Heather and Kira. They have all tolerated my enthusiastic taking of pictures of architecture wherever we travel together.

This book fulfills another bucket list item for me, and it is dedicated to my family as a heartfelt thank you for their continued love and support.

Expect the Best,

DISTINCTIVE Homes OF AMERICA™

NAPLES, FLORIDA
COLLIER COUNTY

Aqualane Shores & Royal Harbor

Waldorf Astoria

PRODUCED BY
©Distinctive Homes of America

About this book

The "Distinctive Homes of America" book presents fifty incredible homes in over 700 full-color photographs, located from as far north as Mediterra to the southern most point of Port Royal by Gordon Pass. Each home was selected because of its unique features that set it apart from the ordinary. Some homes are so well designed and constructed, they are without peer.

Our goal was to present these fifty homes and their surrounding communities to give you, the viewer a sense of actually being there. Twelve professional photographers contributed their own spectacular work to accomplish this. The principle photography was shot by author Glenn Hettinger, AIA as he drove, boated and walked all around Naples.

Most of the homes are arranged in random order to avoid a repetition of architectural style, designers, builders or neighborhoods. This also creates a sense of anticipation with each page turn. Please enjoy your personal tour of these homes, many of which have not previously been photographed.

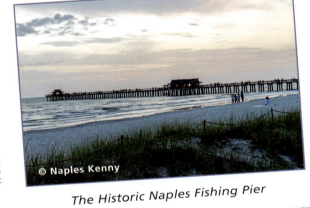

The Historic Naples Fishing Pier

Naples

Basking in tropical sun on the southwest side of Florida, Naples' white sandy beaches are beautifully decorated with shells from the Gulf of Mexico. It has an abundance of calm seas, bays and inlets welcoming boaters, fishermen and recreationists. Friends and neighbors regularly meet on the beach to watch the magnificent sunsets.

The streets are lushly landscaped with tropical palms and flowering trees. Its natural stunning beauty and serenity is a perfect backdrop to its distinctive architecture. Naples has incredible world-class shopping and dining districts, and is home to some of the most luxurious waterfront and golf course estates in the world.

In fact, Naples has the world record for the most golf courses per capita. If you like golf, you will love Naples – where eagles, cranes, alligators and other wildlife abound.

Naples is in Collier County which has about 330,000 residents. It is south of Ft. Myers, north of Marco Island and a 120 mile drive west on 'Alligator Alley' from Miami.

FLORIDA

THE PRISTINE BEAUTY *of* Naples

© Randall Perry

© D. Thompson

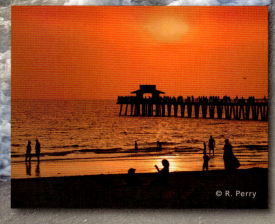
© R. Perry

© G. Hettinger

THE EXPERIENCE OF
Gulf Coast Living

"Visiting Naples for the first time was love at first sight for me. I had lived in Florida for 32 years, but it took traveling to a destination wedding in April, 2013 for me to discover Naples. I was amazed by all of the things that I loved about this town, and I instantly knew that it would make a great setting for my next book – this one.

Naples had a wide variety of gorgeous homes in many different styles and settings. They are plentiful from the southern tip at Gordon Pass to the northern tip at Barefoot Beach. In addition to my subject of single-family homes, there were many beautiful condominium towers, townhouses and apartments. All of which had a backdrop of pristine waterways and lush tropical landscaping, with great weather to boot.

This community had all of the amenities that one would expect in a much bigger city. The shopping districts and accompanying dining were world class, as were the recreational amenities. I'm not even a golfer, and yet I loved being around all of the beautifully landscaped golf courses. And as much as I enjoyed driving around town seeking 'Distinctive Homes,' it was when I took to the water that I fell in love all over again, with the whole place. The Gulf of Mexico along with unique inlets and bays, make for a fabulous boating excursion, and fishing is always superb.

One contagious custom is the flow of pedestrians heading west to the white sandy beaches, every night about an hour before sunset. The east-west avenues are filled with residents carrying beach chairs and refreshments. This town makes time to enjoy the free sunsets with neighbors and a cold drink most evenings. You just have to experience it to be reminded of the simple pleasures and how wonderful it is to live on the 'gentle side of Florida.'"

— Author, Glenn D. Hettinger

CONTENTS

PAGE   **DESCRIPTION**

PAGE		DESCRIPTION
14		"What Makes a Home Distinctive?"
16	HOME 1	2011 — Old Florida — *"Sterling Silver"*
22	HOME 2	2007 — Contemporary Classical Revival
28	HOME 3	1970, Remodel 2011 — West Indies, Organic Modern — *"Beach Haven"*
32	HOME 4	2007 — California Mission — *"Villa Cantera"*
36	HOME 5	2012 — Key West with French Interior — *"Le Cadeau Sur La Gulf"*
40	HOME 6	2011 to 2014 — Key West Revival — *"Gables on Sixth"*
42	HOME 7	2011 to 2014 — Key West Revival — *"Gables on Sixth"*
43	HOME 8	2011 to 2014 — Key West Revival — *"Gables on Sixth"*
44	HOME 9	2011 to 2014 — Key West Revival — *"Gables on Sixth"*
45	HOME 10	2011 to 2014 — Key West Revival — *"Gables on Sixth"*
46	HOME 11	2011 to 2014 — Key West Revival — *"Gables on Sixth"*
47	HOME 12	2011 to 2014 — Key West Revival — *"Gables on Sixth"*
48	HOME 13	2011 — Classic Parisian Renaissance
52	HOME 14	2011 — Colonial Plantation — *"Vie de la Mer"*
56	HOME 15	2007-2009 — Classical Mediterranean Estate
62	HOME 16	2014 — Contemporary Dutch Colonial
66	HOME 17	2012 — New Orleans French Plantation — *"Lady Pontalba"*
70	HOME 18	1925, Remodel 2008-2010 — Key West Cottage — *"Southern Belle"*
75	HOME 19	2008 — Bermuda/Dutch Island
78	HOME 20	2011 — Authentic Old Florida Revival
82	HOME 21	2013 — Old Florida Coastal Cottage
86	HOME 22	2009 — French Cottage by the Sea — *"Maison du Bonheur"*
89	HOME 23	2006 — Charleston Coastal — *"Southern Comfort"*
92	HOME 24	1921, Additions 1992, 2002 & 2013 — Historic Florida Cottage — *"Cuidado con el Perro"*
96	HOME 25	2009 — Old Florida
100	HOME 26	2005 — Caribbean Island Estate

CONTENTS

PAGE   **DESCRIPTION**

104	HOME 27	2009 — Island & Low Country Plantation
108	HOME 28	2014 — Tuscan Estate — *"Piccola Villaggio"*
114	HOME 29	2013 — Classic Florida Revival
118	HOME 30	2006, Remodel 2014 — Whimsical Arts and Crafts — *"Mermaid Memories"*
122	HOME 31	2010 — Tropical West Indies
126	HOME 32	2009 — Formal Mediterranean
130	HOME 33	2011 — Old Florida with Nantucket Flair — *"La Playa"*
136	HOME 34	2006 — French Country Estate — *"Lookout"*
142	HOME 35	2005 — Georgian Island — *"The Four Treasures"*
146	HOME 36	2004 — British West Indies — *"Winsome"*
152	HOME 37	2013 — West Indies to Transitional Contemporary — *"Barefoot Beach"*
154	HOME 38	2013 — West Indies to Transitional Contemporary — *"Barefoot Beach"*
155	HOME 39	2013 — West Indies to Transitional Contemporary — *"Barefoot Beach"*
156	HOME 40	2013 — West Indies to Transitional Contemporary — *"Barefoot Beach"*
158	HOME 41	1999 — Colonial Plantation
162	HOME 42	2010 — New Age Mediterranean Revival — *"Montelena"*
166	HOME 43	1991, Remodel 2014 — Bermuda Island — *"Happy House"*
170	HOME 44	2001 — French Country
173	HOME 45	2006, Remodel 2013 — French Caribbean Plantation — *"Home in the Sky"*
178	HOME 46	2004 — Italian Mediterranean Estate
181	HOME 47	2011 — French Country Estate
186	HOME 48	1994 — Italian Whimsical Naples — *"Pasa del Sol"*
191	HOME 49	2013 — Old Florida & Coastal Caribbean
194	HOME 50	1985, Remodel 2001 — Key West Victorian Estate — *"The Happy House"*
200	THIRTY-NINE MORE HOMES of DISTINCTION	
206	GREEN BUILDING INITIATIVES & ENERGY-EFFICIENT DESIGN	
208	TWENTY-SEVEN DISTINCTIVE MAILBOXES	
216	DISTINCTIVE GUIDE	

WHAT MAKES A HOME
DISTINCTIVE?

Glenn Hettinger

What does Webster's Dictionary say?

DISTINCTIVE: *adj.*
Serving to distinguish or set apart from others.

DISTINCT: *adj.*
1. Distinguishable from all others.
2. Easily perceived; clear.
3. Clearly defined; unquestionable.

What does the author say?
Distinctive is used here to indicate homes with unique character, typically designed by an architect as one-of-a-kind. If you invested weeks of driving, walking and boating around Naples, as I did, these homes would stand out as being different in a positive way. A few are included more for their uniqueness, but most are award-winning designs, spectacular, and/or grand. Together they provide a plethora of home design ideas and details worth imitating.

How were the 50 "Distinctive Homes of America," Volume III — Naples, FL chosen?
The number one common thread is that all 50 homes look great and look like they were designed by a talented architect. All 50 homes are tastefully designed with sensitivity to their client's program, site constraints, timing, budget, and attention to proportions and details.

Other considerations included: Were they considered the most beautiful homes? …the best designed homes? …the best representative of a certain architectural style? …the most unique homes? …or the homes with the most unusual history?

How was Naples, FL chosen for this type of book?
It is a beautiful community that has a wide variety of distinctive homes. The shores of the Gulf and inlets have an attractive mix of Palladian, Mediterranean, Craftsman, Contemporary, Beach & Tropical Cottage and Classic Revival styles. Home sizes vary on purpose from large estates to small cottages. Home sites are mostly flat but range from waterfront to interior sites. Home ages stretch over many years. In short, it is a target rich environment of photogenic subjects for this type of lavishly-illustrated tabletop book.

Why are there 50 featured homes in the book?
While Naples, FL is rich with hundreds of "Distinctive Homes," the author chose to limit this book to 50 homes to allow enough pages to present each home. By one perspective, 50 homes give the reader a lot to look at. But, by another perspective only 50 homes out of thousands in a prestigious community is exclusive company.

Why were some other homes not included?
Some other homes may have appeared in this book if: 1.) The author had discovered them; 2.) The view angles for quality photographs were more accessible; 3.) The home had been completed and ready to be photographed by July, 2014; or 4.) The home owners had agreed for their home to be included.

How were the 700 photographs obtained?
The goal is to use the best images available. The author is the principal photographer taking about half of the photographs and the other half were contributed by 14 other terrific professional photographers. All of these professional images are very welcomed and the contributing photographers are credited on each printed image and several other places. Any photos taken on private property or interior shots are done with written permission from the homeowners.

How is the Homeowner's Privacy Protected?
No addresses or even home numbers are in the book, and each homeowner decides how to identify their home. They can remain completely anonymous, use only the name of the home, use their sir name or full names – they decide. They also approve their entire home layout before the book goes to press.

DISTINCTIVE HOME I

"Sterling Silver"

Owners – "This is the first home that we commissioned. We wanted a family oriented home that was cozy, yet state-of-the-art and elegant. We also wanted a fun home and we love the casual aspects that make it very 'livable.' But it also had to be energy-efficient and environmentally friendly. We think that the LEED Silver indicates that we got that too."

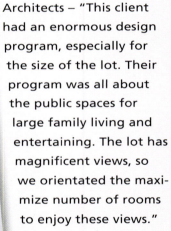

Architects – "This client had an enormous design program, especially for the size of the lot. Their program was all about the public spaces for large family living and entertaining. The lot has magnificent views, so we orientated the maximize number of rooms to enjoy these views."

DESCRIPTION / RESOURCES		
BUILT	2011	
TOTAL AREA	8,800 SF on 2 Levels	
STYLE	Old Florida	
ARCHITECT	Stofft Cooney Architects - Naples, FL	
BUILDER	BCB Homes - Naples, FL	
INTERIOR DESIGN	CK Interior Design - Denver, CO	
CABINETRY	AlliKristé Fine Cabinetry & Kitchen Design - Naples, FL	
LANDSCAPE ARCHITECT	Exteriors by Koby Kirwin - Naples, FL	
WINDOWS	Weather Shield Windows - Medord, WI	
LEED CONSULTANTS	E3 Building Sciences - Bonita Springs, FL	
RECOGNITION	*Florida Architecture* Magazine 84th Edition - Cover LEED Silver Certified	
PHOTOGRAPHY	Lori Hamilton Photography & Glenn Hettinger, AIA	

"The lot was tight with lot coverage and height restrictions, but the team still produced an excellent piece of architecture that lives well. All of the extra energy efficiencies that were part of the LEED program just added to the distinctiveness of this home."

LEED SILVER CERTIFIED ENERGY EFFICIENT HOME
For more details see pages 210-211

Builder – "BCB Homes' President/CEO, Joe Smallwood, invested time researching some of the green products and learning about their features for this distinctive home."

Interior Designer —
"The interiors have been designed as a place to entertain friends and family. For this particular client, it was important to focus on practicality & efficiency while trying to keep a consistent Old Florida style design throughout."

"I had a lot of fun working with the owners and the subcontractors for this home. And now we have experience with a lot of new products that we can use in future BCB homes."

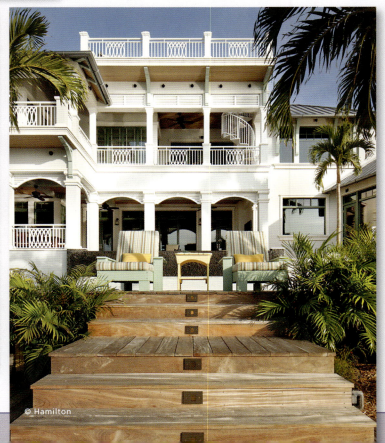

DISTINCTIVE HOME II

Owners – "We desired to mix classical and contemporary elements into our own unique home. We think that the design team achieved our goals, because our home is quite functional and makes us feel good just living in it. We're glad that the author found it to be distinctive and wanted to include it in his book."

Architect – "We wanted to maximize the availability of natural light and views from both sides of the main interior volume. So we used a sophisticated and symmetrically organized home design with clean contemporary lines and an H-shape plan layout."

DESCRIPTION / RESOURCES		
BUILT	2007	
TOTAL AREA	8,500 SF on 2 Levels	
STYLE	Contemporary Classical Revival	
ARCHITECT	Kukk Architecture & Design, P.A. - Naples, FL	
INTERIOR BUILDER	Thomas Riley Artisan's Guild - Naples, FL	
INTERIOR DESIGN	Chandra L. Payne Interior Design - Dallas, TX	
CABINETRY	Thomas Riley Artisan's Guild - Naples, FL	
LANDSCAPE DESIGN	Owner & David Larson - Dallas, TX	
WINDOWS	Hope's Windows, Inc. - Jamestown, NY	
RECOGNITION	*Architectural* Magazine; Hope's Window ads; The Robb Report	
PHOTOGRAPHY	Sargent Architectural Photography & Glenn Hettinger, AIA	

"The main space features a diffused skylight crowning a vaulted tray ceiling further adding to the day-lighting effectiveness. This main space acts as the hub for a fairly strict symmetry in both plan and elevation. Inside the main living space, aligned and flanking fireplaces backed by gunmetal over mantles act as bookends within the space. Twin garages with second floor VIP suites embrace the front."

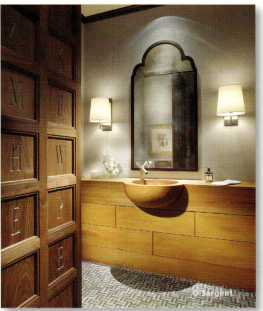

middle & right: 'His and hers' powder rooms each with its own unique character and artwork align both sides of the foyer entry.

"Specially prepared and polished concrete panels clad the exterior of the home and blend with the slate roofing to create a neutral color palette. Contrasting with the earth tones is the multicolored glass tile water basin and lap pool with spillways expanding out to the bay views beyond. A trellis colonnade defines the upper terrace and provides both a sense of place and a welcome relief from the sun."

DISTINCTIVE HOME III

"Beach Haven"
THE HAMPEL HOME

Owners – "We wanted an interior that would capture both our worldly and beach-chic lifestyles. We love living adjacent to the beach, and the ability to watch the sunsets from our balcony. We also enjoy having a very large salt water pool."

DESCRIPTION / RESOURCES		
	BUILT	1970s Ranch; 2011 Major Addition
	TOTAL AREA	5,183 SF on 2 Levels
	STYLE	West Indies - Organic Modern
	ARCHITECT	Architecture Artistica, Inc. - Ft. Myers, FL
	BUILDER	Old Naples Builders, Inc. - Naples, FL
	INTERIOR DESIGN	Jalan Jalan Collection, Inc. - Miami, FL
	CABINETRY	Tradewind Designs, Inc. - Naples, FL
	MILLWORK & BUILT-INS	Old Naples Builders, Inc. - Naples, FL
	WINDOWS	Marvin Windows & Doors
	TILE & MARBLE	Alpha Stone Designs - Naples, FL
	POOL	Nassau Pools Construction, Inc. - Naples, FL
	RECOGNITION	*Design District* Mag. - Summer 2012 cover story
	PHOTOGRAPHY	Dana Hoff Photographer & Glenn Hettinger, AIA

above: Naples own artist, Ed Koehler created the large sculpture of a driftwood wall sconce enhanced by the dark chocolate brown wall behind it.

top: The foyer sports a flanking pair of Mother-of-pearl and bone mirrors from Syria.

Architect – "Our client asked that we incorporate the original nondescript 1970's ranch home into the planning of a state-of-the-art home more than three times its size. They wanted features of Old Florida architecture with a touch of the islands."

Author's award for most Distinctive Mailbox.

Jack, the perfect Papillon

above: At the end of the swimming pool there is a free standing root sculpture on a stainless steel base that is completely supported by its own weight.

Interior Designer – "Our clients wanted a relaxing organic yet modern environment. Warm woods and colorful accents punctuate the soft color palette."

Builder – "We built this home with all of the best finishes. It also has a one touch lighting system controlled by the owner's computer or phone."

far left: The kitchen includes Subzero, Wolf and Miele stainless steel appliances, with Vermont soapstone counters and Carrera mosaic back-splashes. The island has a gorgeous slab of Carrera Calcutta marble while travertine marble and Waterworks tiles complete the baths.

DISTINCTIVE HOME IV

"Villa Cantera"

Owners/Builders – "When we met with the architect it was important for Steve to have as many garages as possible without seeing them from the front.

We also wanted it to look like the house had been there forever. Thus the four car garage in the back and one car garage in the front that is closer and more convenient to the kitchen."

"We wanted an additional bedroom on the first floor for our grandchildren so they wouldn't feel so far from the master bedroom. Upstairs we decided to include two spacious bedroom suites for comfort and privacy of our visiting family or guests. These formed the basis for design from which we began."

DESCRIPTION / RESOURCES		
BUILT	2007	
TOTAL AREA	5,400 SF on 2 Levels	
STYLE	California Mission	
ARCHITECT	Stofft Cooney Architects - Naples, FL	
BUILDER	Foresite Homes - Naples, FL	
INTERIOR DECOR	Kathleen Cantera - Naples, FL	
LANDSCAPE & POOL DESIGN	Exteriors by Koby Kirwin - Naples, FL	
WINDOWS	Weathershield Windows and Doors	
AUTOMATION	Ambiance Aduio of Naples	
PHOTOGRAPHY	Tom Harper Photography & Glenn Hettinger, AIA	

"We didn't want a two story foyer open to the upstairs but a cozy comfortable feel with the view of the pool. We also wanted to have the kitchen, family and dining rooms all open without feeling too big or too small. I love the size of the home, and I love the cozy feel of coming home."

Architect – "This home is deceiving in that it is much bigger than it looks from the street. The owners wanted a fairly formal hacienda look built around a pool. We created the views of the ample courtyard and beautifully tiled pool."

© Harper

© Harper

© Hettinger

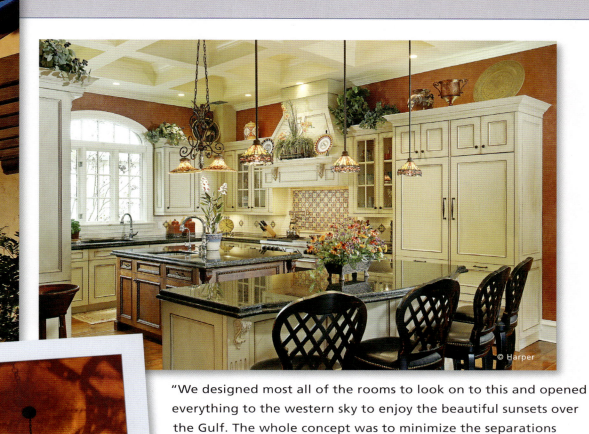

"We designed most all of the rooms to look on to this and opened everything to the western sky to enjoy the beautiful sunsets over the Gulf. The whole concept was to minimize the separations between indoor and outdoor living. And we used many authentic details that the owners had collected in their travel photos."

Interior Decor – "The Owner's wanted their home to have a Mediterranean feel with more of the Spanish influence. So, we used Mexican tile and Mexican sinks. The Mexican tile surrounds the windows in the front, in the kitchen and around the pool and hot tub. But there we used the tile in a Moroccan type of design. We also used Moroccan light fixtures and colors in the Master Bedroom and Italian faux paint and arches throughout the house. The lighted niches came from the villas in St. Lucia where they stayed many times."

DISTINCTIVE HOME V

"Le Cadeau Sur La Gulf"
(The Gift on the Gulf)
THE BECTON-READ HOME

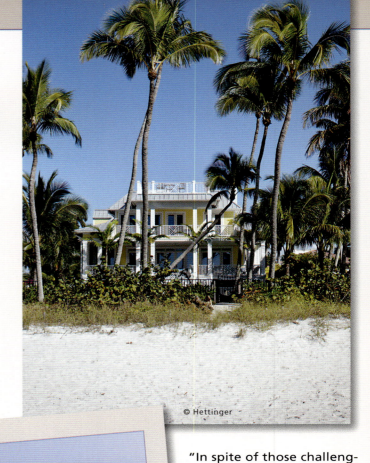
© Hettinger

Owners – "We might have the most photographed home in Naples. And it comes complete with views of the Gulf and the Naples Pier. …Due to an unusual set of circumstances, our interior became an adaptation of Versailles."

Architect – "The biggest challenge in designing this distinctive home was the site restrictions. The lot has two different front setbacks, a rear yard that is actually the side property line and a side yard that looked onto the Gulf beaches and Naples Pier. On top of that was a maximum height as well as an 'Angle of Light' massing restriction."

"In spite of those challenges we were able to create a home whose exterior evoked the Old Florida styling reminiscent of nearby historic cottages. Each room in this long narrow plan still has a view of the Gulf. A wonderful highlight is the easily accessible rooftop viewing deck."

DESCRIPTION / RESOURCES		
BUILT	2012	
TOTAL AREA	12,000 SF on 3 Levels	
STYLE	Key West with French Interior	
HOME DESIGNER	The Sater Group, Inc. - Bonita Springs, FL	
G.C.	Grand Bay Building & Development - Naples, FL	
INTERIOR DESIGN	Lizabeth Becton-Read with Canada Design Group - Naples, FL	
CABINETRY	Xavier's Collection Fine Cabinetry, Inc. - Naples, FL	
LANDSCAPE ARCHITECT	Windham Studio, Inc. - Naples, FL	
LANDSCAPE MANAGEMENT	Renfroe & Jackson, Inc. - Naples, FL	
COASTAL ENGINEER	Humiston & Moore Engineers - Naples, FL	
POOL	Serenity Pool & Spa - Bonita Springs, FL	
WINDOWS	Andersen 400 Series Storm Watch - Naples, FL	
AUTOMATION	Lutron Lighting - Naples, FL	
RECOGNITION	Naples Botanical Gardens Tour 2013	
PHOTOGRAPHY	Keith Isaac Photography & Naples Kenny Photography & Glenn Hettinger, AIA	

Interior Designer – "The surprising formality of the French interior is offset by the simplicity of the exterior. The two are blended together so eloquently. The marble front steps and fleur de lis on the leaded glass entrance doors hint at what one may find once they enter the home. A custom stone medallion is centered on the floor of the gilded grand foyer.

Builder – "This home, with its proximity to the beach, brought about challenges from a builder's perspective. After working through those challenges, we feel we were able to give the homeowner the house of her dreams."

"The halls are lined with Schonbek chandeliers. The kitchen showcases the Gulf of Mexico, and hand painted French tile murals. The master suite, which is gilded in silver, houses a hand painted breakfast bar sink and French bathroom cabinetry. These are just a few of the elements this special home has to offer."

"Having spent a portion of her childhood in Paris, she wanted to incorporate Louis the XIV design into the project. The marriage of the exterior and the interior of this home is what makes it such a uniquely distinctive home."

DISTINCTIVE HOMES
VI, VII, VIII, IX, X, XI & XII

"The Gables on Sixth"

Author – "I was exploring Naples and discovered seven distinctive homes on the same block – each different, but fitting beautifully together. They were all by the same developer. Five were designed by one architect and two by a different architect. Walking in front of all seven homes is a delight."

HOME VI

Developer – "The Gables was certainly a challenge as it was the first project of its kind in this area. The planning process was a considerable undertaking, but the end result was well worth the effort and is now being duplicated all over the downtown area. The homes look like they have been in place for years, and each design compliments the next."

DESCRIPTION / RESOURCES		
BUILT	2011 to 2014	
TOTAL AREA	2,800 SF - 3,400 SF on 2 Levels	
STYLE	Key West Revival	
ARCHITECT #1 for 5 Homes	Harrell & Company Architects - Naples, FL	
ARCHITECT #2 for 2 Homes	MHK Architecture & Planning - Naples, FL	
BUILDER	Naples Redevelopment, Inc. - Naples, FL	
INTERIOR DESIGN	Kelly Goodsey Design, Inc. - (all specs) & Mary Cooney - 1 home & Jennifer Marchionda - 1 home all Naples, FL	
LANDSCAPE & POOL DESIGN	GardenBleu Landscape Architecture - Naples, FL	
WINDOWS	Andersen 400 Series, Storm Watch - Naples, FL	
AUTOMATION	Ambiance Security Systems - Naples, FL	
RECOGNITION	Florida Design; *Home & Design* 2014 Resource Guide; Grandeur Mag. Fall 2013	
PHOTOGRAPHY	Lori Hamilton Photography & Glenn Hettinger, AIA	

SEVEN HOMES FROM THE GABLES ON SIXTH

DISTINCTIVE HOMES
VI, VII, VIII, IX, X, XI & XII

"The Gables on Sixth"

"We strove to create timeless designs in a very central location and placed great emphasis on the elevations with the cedar beam fascia, gable fronts and shingle facing, Azak columns, and abundant landscaping with full size trees and plantings."

HOME VII

HOME VIII

DISTINCTIVE HOMES
VI, VII, VIII, IX, X, XI & XII

"The Gables on Sixth"

Architect #1 – "The site configuration is very different from many in Old Naples - long narrow sites with an alley behind. This is reminiscent of original town planning after the automobile became commonplace, but before the garage became a dominant element."

HOME IX

HOME X

DISTINCTIVE HOMES
VI, VII, VIII, IX, X, XI & XII

"The Gables on Sixth"

"Having done a lot of work in historic Key West, the scale and charm of Key West vernacular seemed to fit that required on this project since the garage does not dominate the façade. We explored the evolution of Key West vernacular."

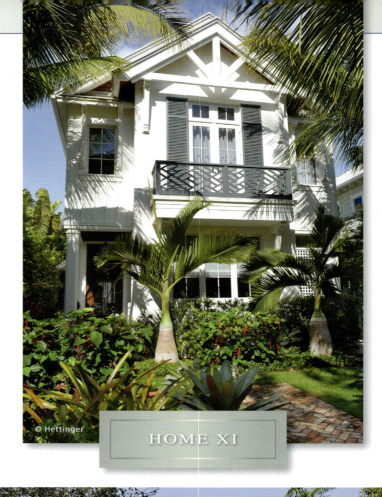

HOME XI

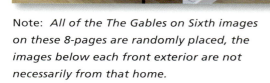

Note: All of the The Gables on Sixth images on these 8-pages are randomly placed, the images below each front exterior are not necessarily from that home.

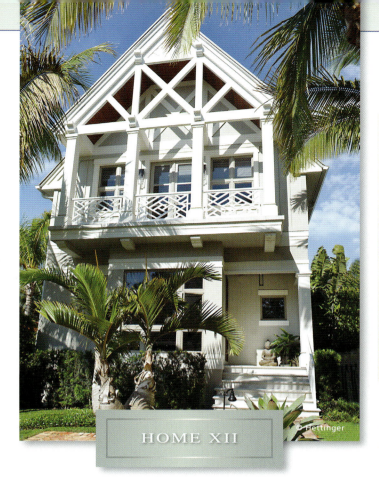

HOME XII

"We maintained the scale and whimsical character of Key West while adapting the floor plan to current lifestyles. The result is exterior architecture with charm and character that flows into a light filled interior and open plan concept that most owners now prefer."

DISTINCTIVE HOME XIII

THE MARTIN HOME

Owners – "We have enjoyed our home tremendously. Steps from the beach and steps from the finest Naples restaurants. We couldn't have a better location for our family. We love the activity all around. Our children are able to walk out our front door for a swim in the gulf or a gourmet ice cream cone. When we want privacy our pool is flanked by plush walls of landscaping that keeps us shielded from the outside world. Everything at our fingertips is what our home has given us and we love it! We feel very fortunate to live here."

Architect/ Builder – "The site, an 'in town' parcel of limited proportions, adjacent to the shops and restaurants of 5th Avenue...

DESCRIPTION / RESOURCES		
BUILT	2012	
TOTAL AREA	8,000 SF on 3 Levels	
STYLE	Classic Parisian Renaissance	
ARCHITECT	Eugene E. Martin, AIA - Naples, FL	
BUILDER	Martin Custom Homes, Inc. - Naples, FL	
INTERIOR DESIGN	Homeowner with Tay Ruthenburg - Evansville, IN	
CABINETRY	AlliKriste Kitchens - Naples, FL	
LANDSCAPE ARCHITECT	Isaacson Landscape Architecture Group - Naples, FL	
WINDOWS	Weather Shield Windows & Doors - Medford, WI	
AUTOMATION	Ambiance Audio Design & Security, Inc. - Naples, FL	
PHOTOGRAPHY	Glenn Hettinger, AIA	

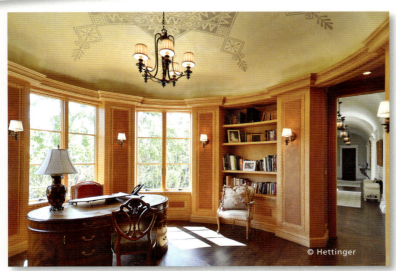

"...with elevated views of the Gulf of Mexico, dictated the townhouse style."

"Regulations dictated that the first living level would be elevated to protect against a tidal surge. But that actually elevated the roof enough to have a nice roof terrace with a hot tub from which to view the sunsets over the Gulf. The owner's affection for classic Parisian architecture led to the balanced formal elevations clad in sculpted marble and forged ironwork."

Interior Designer – "Having an architect as a husband I quickly realized we would have many houses we would call home. I needed a style that could adapt easily in many different settings. A style that made transitioning effortless for my family. Twenty years ago our interior designer chose pieces we still love today. That's the beauty of working with Tay, he has an eye for beauty today that remains timeless. Each time we move we add a little here and there to spruce things up, but the core feeling remains and a house becomes another home for us immediately."

DISTINCTIVE HOME XIV

"Vie de la Mer"
(Life of the Sea)

Owners – "We love the unique and timeless architectural design of our home. All exterior and interior elements present such character and charm."

Architect – "The client desired a warm, understated look not characterized in the latest design trends."

"We introduced some rustic elements of European architecture found in corners of the tropics which could suggest 'Colonial Plantation.' The prevailing flood zone required an elevated pool which became a design centerpiece. The pool creates the soothing sound of a water wall just beyond the lower entry gates."

DESCRIPTION / RESOURCES		
BUILT	2011	
TOTAL AREA	5,000 SF on 3 Levels	
STYLE	Colonial Plantation	
ARCHITECT	Harrell & Company Architects - Naples, FL	
BUILDER	BCB Homes - Naples, FL	
INTERIOR DESIGN	Romanza Interior Design - Naples, FL	
CABINETRY	Tradewinds Designs, Inc. - Naples, FL	
LANDSCAPE ARCHITECT	Garden Bleu Landscape Architecture - Naples, FL	
POOL DESIGN	Garden Bleu Landscape Architecture - Naples, FL	
WINDOWS	Weather Shield Windows - Medford, WI	
RECOGNITION	*Southwest Florida Home & Design* 2012 - Sand Dollar Award for Best Pool Design	
PHOTOGRAPHY	Lori Hamilton Photography	

"It becomes an eye level reflecting pool at the elevated main living areas to further the Southern Caribbean imagery. Elevated living spaces provide privacy and help capture the Gulf beach breezes only steps away. The quaint character recalls a sleepier, yet more eccentric time in southwest Florida."

Interior Designer – "Senior Designer, Michael Scott worked very closely with the owners to develop a clear direction with respect to the overall design theme of the home. Complementary elements of traditional fabrics and textures were interwoven with more modern accessories, lighting, and finishes blending the old and the new for a fresh, 'transitional' atmosphere. The Turkish Travertine flooring and beige walls create a warm palette for an inviting living space."

DISTINCTIVE HOME XV

Architect – "This client had researched our work and they liked everything that we had designed. So they gave us a free rein with very little interaction. The home was designed around the Gulf views and there were few site challenges because the site was a large one. We achieved Gulf views in most rooms except the VIP guest suite out front."

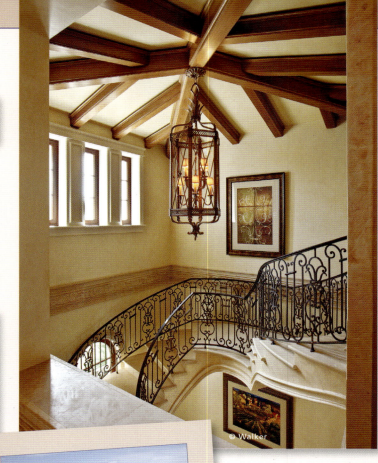

"So we added cantilevered balconies with Mizner-influenced heavy timber details and an entrance water feature for a view. There's a high level of finishes with mahogany windows, copper gutters, lots of carved stone, etc."

DESCRIPTION / RESOURCES		
	BUILT	2007-2009
	TOTAL AREA	Unlisted SF on 3 Levels
	STYLE	Classical Mediterranean Estate
	ARCHITECT	Stofft Cooney Architects - Naples, FL
	BUILDER	Kurtz Homes Naples - Naples, FL
	INTERIOR DESIGN	Decorators Unlimited, Inc. - Palm Beach Gardens, FL
	CABINETRY	C&C WoodWorking, LLC - formerly Baker's CC - Naples, FL
	LANDSCAPE & POOL DESIGN	Belk Pool Design - Naples. FL
	AUTOMATION	AMX - panels & theater; Executive Electronics - full security
	PHOTOGRAPHY	C.J. Walker Photography & Glenn Hettinger, AIA

Interior Designer – "We were fortunate to be on this great design team. The home has authentic Mediterranean accents on the exterior and we followed that lead on the interior design. We used real, hand carved stone jambs and columns."

"Each bedroom had a different theme and we detailed all of the distinctive ceiling treatments. We kept the formal rooms very formal and toned it down as rooms got more informal. We even used the 'vibrant island colors' on the veranda furniture because of the many coconut palms in the views that inspired us."

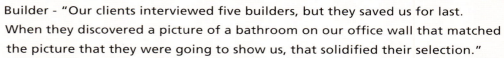

Builder - "Our clients interviewed five builders, but they saved us for last. When they discovered a picture of a bathroom on our office wall that matched the picture that they were going to show us, that solidified their selection."

"Everything about the construction is top quality materials and craftsmanship. We built a marble entrance with custom water jetted patterns in it. We used a bamboo ceiling in the 'Tommy Bahama like guest room' and a herring bone copper ceiling in the study. When people ask me about my favorite homes, I don't think as much about the home as I do the clients and the relationship; and this is one of those that I liked best."

DISTINCTIVE HOME XVI

THE GLEN & ROBYNN LERNER HOME

Owners – "Because of its location one block from the Gulf, we wanted a house that felt like a beach house but also had some architectural flair. The design by Matt Kragh and Adam Smith let them fit a lot of living into the smaller lots of Old Naples."

DESCRIPTION / RESOURCES		
	BUILT	2014
	TOTAL AREA	6,000 SF on 2 Levels
	STYLE	Contemporary Dutch Colonial
	ARCHITECT	MHK Architecture & Planning - Naples, FL
	BUILDER	Naples Redevelopment, Inc. - Naples, FL
	INTERIOR DESIGN	Kelly Godsey Design, Inc. & Robynn Lerner - Naples, FL
	CABINETRY	Downsview Kitchens & Robynn Lerner - Naples, FL
	LANDSCAPE ARCHITECT	Architectural Land Design, Inc. - Naples, FL
	WINDOWS	Andersen 400 Series - Storm Watch - Naples, FL
	FEATURE DOOR	Solar Innovations, Inc. - Pine Grove, PA
	AUTOMATION	Control 4 and Vantage
	PHOTOGRAPHY	Glenn Hettinger, AIA

"Because the house has no hallways and no formal living or dining room, they were still able to get 5 large bedrooms, 5 full baths, 2 half baths, an office, a home theater and a custom hot yoga room into a space that took over 10,000 feet when we lived in Arizona. We realized that in the three years living in our AZ home we never used our formal living room and only used the formal dining room three times. Our home now lives so open and it just feels like a beach house should."

Architect - "This home was one of those amazing projects where the client gave us direction on style and size and said create a timeless masterpiece. The home, boasting an extravagant flow and openness, was designed around those four glorious seasonal months for Naples."

"It is built around an amazing pool that interacts with the house from every angle. It's the kind of home you want to hang around in your swimsuit all day."

Interior Designer – "We all worked together and took a modern and simplistic approach with this distinctive home. The design elements consisted of straight and simple lines. We wanted the home to be modern with a nice beachy feel. We used white backgrounds to compliment the Lerner's contemporary art collection and the warm grey custom wood floors."

DISTINCTIVE HOME XVII

"Lady Pontalba"

Owners – "The Baroness de Pontalba was a wealthy New Orleans Aristocrat business woman and real estate developer with a dynamic personality. The Pontalba buildings in New Orleans are in the French Quarter. The railings around our home are reminiscent of the railings seen on these very famous New Orleans buildings."

Architect – "The most exciting part of designing a custom home of this magnitude is working with a client and builder that are just as excited about the project as we are. Knowing that in the end, the result will be well worth the additional efforts that all members of each team has put forth. The biggest reward is seeing the excitement in the homeowners eyes, knowing they can now call this incredible structure, home."

BUILT	2012	
TOTAL AREA	6,500 SF on 3 Levels	
STYLE	New Orleans French Plantation	
ARCHITECT	Weber Design Group, Inc. - Naples, FL	
G.C.	Grand Bay Building & Devel. Corp. - Naples, FL	
INTERIOR DESIGN	Kathleen Maier with Brenda Canada & Traditions - Naples, FL Chez Del - Akron, OH; Calico Corners	
CABINTRY	Xavier's Collection Fine Cabinetry, Inc. - Naples, FL	
LANDSCAPE DESIGN	Renfroe & Jackson, Inc. - Naples, FL	
POOL CONSTRUCTION	Serenity Pool & Spa - Bonita Springs, FL	
WINDOWS	Andersen 400 Series, Storm Watch	
DOCKS	Garland & Garland Marine Construction - Naples, FL	
RECOGNITION	Naples Garden Club Home Tour Naples Women's Club Kitchen Tour	
PHOTOGRAPHY	Keith Isaac Photography & Glenn Hettinger, AIA	

Interior Designers – "We wanted a fresh distinctive look in Naples and have always loved the architecture of New Orleans. We envisioned a home that would reflect our interest in French and Asian design reflecting our travels in France and Asia. The interior design is a mix of Asian and French showing a collection of items from those travels. The idea of creating a warm, comfortable and very inviting atmosphere to go with the trade winds of Florida inspired 'Lady Pontalba.'"

above: Many of the homes in Naples are built on a variety of waterways. And many pools are designed and built to maximize the serenity that comes from looking over a well-designed pool to a natural body of water.

right: This picturesque cottage has been the subject of many artists.

DISTINCTIVE HOME XVIII

"Southern Belle"

THE JOHN & JOYCE FAIN HOME

Owners – "It was love at first sight when we first walked by our cottage. We wanted to maintain the special ambiance of this historical Naples time period, but with low maintenance and high comfort. It is all about hospitality.

We love the spirit of our southern cottage with its effortless charming living close to nature. We have lots of porches and windows to open to the scents and sounds of our environment. And we love walking to everything – the Gulf beach, sunsets, dining and shopping."

DESCRIPTION / RESOURCES	BUILT	1925, Remodeled: 2008-10
	TOTAL AREA	2,100 SF on 2 Levels
	STYLE	Key West Cottage
	ARCHITECT	Unknown
	BUILDER	Remodeling: Gordon Luxury Homes - Naples, FL
	INTERIOR DESIGN	Tillie's Design Co. & Associates - Naples, FL
	LANDSCAPE ARCHITECTURE	Inspired Garden Living, LLC - Naples. FL
	RECOGNITION	Featured in book *'Dream Houses,'* Historic Beach Homes & Cottages of Naples 2011; Cover of 2009 *'The Historic Cottages of Naples'*
	PHOTOGRAPHY	Glenn Hettinger, AIA

Landscape Designer – "The Owner's hospitable and southern demeanor was inspirational to the landscape design. The 'Charlestonesque,' southern charm of the home beckoned for picket fences, window boxes, an arbor, curved cannonball gates, and bricks and bluestone as paving materials. Using Florida tropical plants to create a Charleston-style garden was pure delight."

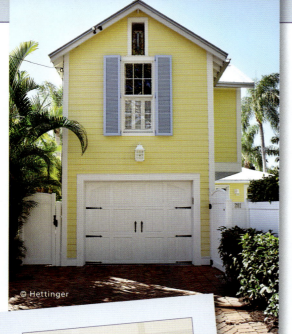

"Flowing, blooming vegetation, hand-crafted urns and trellised vines were incorporated to further emphasize the theme. By staying true to the 'nature of the architecture,' harmony flows between the home and garden."

Author – "This distinctive 1925 Old Naples historic cottage has been luxuriously and charmingly updated to rival any new construction. It has gorgeous reclaimed heart pine floors, tongue-and-groove cypress plank ceilings, cypress cottage board walls, fireplaces in the great room and master bedroom, shell stone floors, copper gutters, etc."

"There's a great front porch and a rear porch overlooking a cascading pool and spa. The charming guest house above the garage is light and spacious with a large bedroom, summer kitchen and private bath."

DISTINCTIVE HOME XIX

Architect – "We started with a beautiful lot with great views. From the start we were designing more to maximize the views rather than to maximize outdoor activities. The clients knew what they wanted and we quickly decided on an authentic Bermuda style with a little Dutch Colonial mixed in. We used an open floor plan, and a lot of pecky cypress."

DESCRIPTION / RESOURCES		
BUILT	2008	
TOTAL AREA	5,500 SF on 2 Levels	
STYLE	Bermuda / Dutch Island	
ARCHITECT	Stofft Cooney Architects - Naples, FL	
BUILDER	Kurtz Homes Naples - Naples, FL	
INTERIOR DESIGN	Stofft Cooney Architects - Naples, FL	
CABINETRY	Baker's Custom Cabinets & Millwork - Naples, FL	
LANDSCAPE & POOL DESIGN	Windham Studio, Inc. - Bonita Springs. FL	
WINDOWS	Andersen Windows & NanaWall Systems, Inc.	
PHOTOGRAPHY	Lori Hamilton Photography & Glenn Hettinger, AIA	

above: A custom desk was made from the same native knotty cypress that was used on the walls.

Builder - "Our clients were experienced homeowners who wanted to replicate several items from their previous homes. They had lots of pictures of details that we emulated. We built a wood bar top similar to the one in their boat. They also wanted the guest bathroom to have the same level of finishes as in their master bath. So we built two fabulous guest master bathrooms. …This water front site had the usual construction challenges. We needed to use concrete pilings under anything that had weight including the pool and the planters."

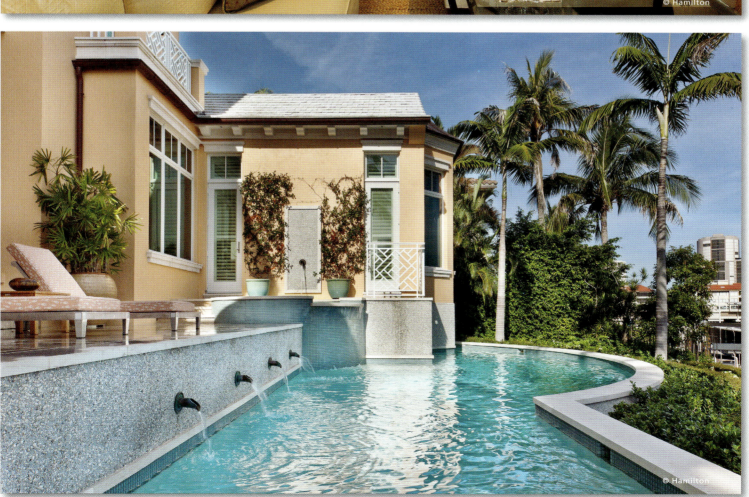

DISTINCTIVE HOME XX

Architects – "Natural light is key to my designs. I like two or three walls of windows everywhere. Despite the narrowness of the Gulf side of the lot all of the bedrooms, even the guest bedrooms still have Gulf views. We used an entry courtyard in the center of the home as an outdoor atrium and angled walls that increased our window opportunities."

"There are great pleasant interior spaces because Sharon has a wonderful knack for designing around the interior architecture and complementing it rather than fighting it."

DESCRIPTION / RESOURCES		
BUILT	2011	
TOTAL AREA	9,000 SF on 3 Levels	
STYLE	Authentic Old Florida Revival	
ARCHITECT	Stofft Cooney Architects - Naples, FL	
BUILDER	Kurtz Homes Naples - Naples, FL	
INTERIOR DESIGN	Montana & Associates - Naples, FL	
OWNERS' REP.	Paul Koening - Stuart, FL	
LANDSCAPE ARCHITECTURE & POOL DESIGN	Exteriors by Koby Kirwin - Naples. FL	
CABINETRY	Busby Cabinets - Gainesville, FL & AliKriste Kitchens - Naples, FL	
AUTOMATION	Lutron Automation	
WINDOWS	Andersen Windows 400 Series Storm Watch - Naples	
RECOGNITION	Featured in *Home & Design* Mag.	
PHOTOGRAPHY	Lori Hamilton Photography; Glenn Hettinger, AIA	

Builder – "The home owners used an owners' rep who had decision making power and that made everything go very smoothly. The architect did a great job of designing such a distinctive home on this narrow lot. There are even upper and lower pools that look like they flow one to another. The owners use this home for family retreats and we had to finish in time for the Mrs.' birthday party. The whole team made the deadline with harmony and we were all invited to the party."

DISTINCTIVE HOME XXI

THE GREG & KRISTEN GRIFFIN HOME

Owners – "We were fortunate to build our home as the first annual '*Home & Design* magazine's Signature Home.' It partnered the magazine with a carefully selected dream team to create the home together."

Home Designer – "This design offers a modern twist on a more traditional floor plan with spaces that flow well together. This is the quintessential Old Naples coastal cottage with charming architectural details such as the dual pitched roof, standing seam metal roof, Bahamian shutters and wide plank horizontal hardy-board siding. Through any number of doorways off the main rooms the view depicts a casual yet stylish approach to alfresco life."

BUILT	2013
TOTAL AREA	4,800 SF on 2 Levels
STYLE	Old Naples Coastal Cottage
HOME DESIGNER	R.G. Designs, Inc. - Bonita Springs, FL
BUILDER	Foresite Homes - Naples, FL
INTERIOR DESIGN	Clive Daniel Home - Naples, FL and *Home & Design* - Naples, FL
CABINETRY	AlliKriste Custom Cabinetry & Kitchen Design - Naples, FL
LANDSCAPE DESIGN	Exteriors by Koby Kirwin - Naples. FL
POOL	Nassau Pools Construction, Inc. - Naples, FL
AUTOMATION	Vitex Home Automation - Naples, FL
WINDOWS	Andersen 400 Series, Storm Watch - Naples, FL
RECOGNITION	First Annual 'Signature Home' in *Home & Design* 2014 - Naples, FL
PHOTOGRAPHY	Giovanni Photography & Glenn Hettinger, AIA

"The view from the formal living room, a perfect example of urban chic, opens to an unobstructed view of the outdoor pool area."

above:
Art: "Coastal Chick" by Leland Brinkman

Interior Design – "The formal dining room features a rusticated farmhouse dining table set against a backdrop of custom carpentry details and hand-crafted columns. Furnishings include a charming mixture of eclectic and 'collected over time' traditional elements, giving the home a casual yet sophisticated design. The expansive outdoor living area features a fireplace extending the comfort of the interiors."

"The Master features a vaulted tongue and groove ceiling and light hardwood floors with a recessed window seat area. The vaulted ceiling carries over into the Bath white marble counter tops along with off-white tile, which highlight the crystal chandelier and oversized driftwood étagère. Truly, every detail chosen has come together in a unique and personalized way."

DISTINCTIVE HOME XXII

"Maison du Bonheur"
(House of Happiness)

Owners – "Although a French country home was our intent, the real inspiration came from a chapel in Dallas that our grandsons attended every morning.

We wanted to reproduce that serene, cozy, welcoming embrace that would cause us to think of our grandsons every day."

right: Builder – "The gigantic timber trusses of the Great Room ceiling, were unique to install because they were actually installed prior to the roof trusses and therefore before the roof went on the home."

"Our project was enhanced because we had lived in Paris for three years and had acquired numerous furnishings and artifacts that easily became the centerpiece of our new home. Along the way, we gathered hundreds of photos and magazine tear sheets and spoke to some of the most interesting people to truly reproduce an authentic French country home by the sea."

DESCRIPTION / RESOURCES		
BUILT	2009	
TOTAL AREA	5,080 SF on 2 Levels	
STYLE	French Cottage by the Sea	
ARCHITECT	Kukk Architecture & Design, P.A. - Naples, FL	
BUILDER	BCB Homes - Naples, FL	
INTERIOR DESIGN	Lorraine McCashin - Naples, FL	
CABINETRY	Tradewind Designs, Inc. - Naples, FL	
WINDOWS	Hurd Windows & Doors - Medford, WI	
RECOGNITION	Naples Illustrated Jan. 2010 - Sand Dollar Award 2009 - Garden Club Tour 2011 Certified Green Home	
PHOTOGRAPHY	Giovanni Photography & Glenn Hettinger, AIA	

Architect – "This 'French Cottage Home' consists of two gabled wings organized around a central vaulted living space. Light filters in from all sides through the creative use of multiple flanking dormers and elegant feature windows in both the upper gable end walls. Strong axial circulation and symmetrical composition abound in the interior spatial organization. The owner's collections of architectural artifacts and antique furnishings are intimately considered and accommodated into the architecture. These personal touches and the daily dance of light within the home combine to create a bright and welcoming place to be."

Builder – "The home owners wanted a durable home that was also certified as a 'Green home.' So, to keep the energy efficiency of the home relatively low, we used Low-E impact glass, Energy Star appliances, a dehumidification system, and Brazilian mahogany wood floors throughout the main living areas of the home."

DISTINCTIVE HOME XXIII

"Southern Comfort"

THE BROWN HOME

Owners – "When we first met with Art Canada of Grand Bay we knew we found someone who had the same passion as us to make our dream home come true. Between the builder and architect we developed a design that will be enjoyed by our family for many years to come. Our goal was to pick up a Charleston classic row home and transplant it in Old Naples. I think we accomplished just that."

"We wanted to make our outdoor covered living space and pool area very usable and unique. The outdoor bath was designed after an outdoor kitchen from the south. Our corner lot became an asset that provided us amble privacy. We could never have accomplished this design on an interior lot."

DESCRIPTION / RESOURCES		
BUILT	2006	
TOTAL AREA	4,110 SF on 2 Levels	
STYLE	Charleston Coastal	
ARCHITECT	Weber Design Group, Inc. - Naples, FL	
BUILDER	Grand Bay Building & Development Corp. - Naples, FL	
INTERIOR DESIGN	EB Designs - Naples, FL	
CABINETRY	Xavier's Collection Fine Cabinetry - Naples, FL	
LANDSCAPE DESIGN	Garden Retreat - Naples, FL	
WINDOWS	PGT Windows & Doors - Miami, FL	
PHOTOGRAPHY	Naples Kenny Photography & Glenn Hettinger, AIA	

Architect – "Our goal with this distinctive home was to create an open and welcoming presentation to a very linear corner lot. These are often times the most challenging lots to work with from a design standpoint. So, in order to give privacy to the outdoor spaces, we created a wraparound veranda on both levels which also assisted in softening the exterior façade."

Architect – "Although the floor plan is narrow, we still wanted it to be flooded with natural light while giving focus to the views from the beautiful and quaint garden and pool areas."

Interior Design – "The interiors reflect an earthy comfort — with warm-wood ceiling and floors throughout — the furniture pieces are surrounded by soft upholstery, punctuated by rustic-wrought iron accents, giving the owners an inviting 'at-home' cozy feel."

DISTINCTIVE HOME XXIV

"Cuidado con el Perro"
(Beware of Dog)

Owners – "We wanted to capture the essence of the Old Naples lifestyle and knew immediately that this historic cottage was where we wanted to be."

"We enlisted the help of an imaginative architect and a very talented landscape designer to help us create what we have today. The combination of indoor and outdoor living areas allows us to enjoy the outstanding in-town location and yet feel secluded in our garden like property."

DESCRIPTION / RESOURCES		
BUILT	1921, Additions: 1992, 2002 & 2013	
TOTAL AREA	3,330 SF on 1 Level	
STYLE	Historic Florida Cottage	
REMODEL ARCHITECT	Andrea Clark Brown Architects, P.A. - Naples, FL	
BUILDERS	The late Al Stiles & Alpha Omega Construction of Naples, Inc. - Naples, FL	
CABINETRY	Workshops of David Smith *(handpainted)*	
LANDSCAPE DESIGN	Jo Ann Smallwood - Naples. FL	
RECOGNITION	Featured in *'Dream Houses,'* Historic Beach Homes and Cottages of Naples 2011	
PHOTOGRAPHY	Naples Kenny Photography & Glenn Hettinger, AIA	

Author – "It is great that this distinctive 1921 landmark cottage continues to be improved rather than removed. It sits is in the heart of Old Naples. It has been luxuriously and charmingly updated to rival any 'new construction.' It has been restored to preserve the charm of the authentic heart pine floors, wood burning fireplace and pecky cypress ceilings."

"The main home has three bedrooms, three baths, wrap-a-round porches and an unusual two-car carport. The gourmet kitchen and baths have been updated with modern amenities. The separate one bedroom, one bathroom guest house features vaulted wood ceilings, a screened porch and a full kitchen for indoor/ outdoor entertaining.

The newest building is the poolside pavilion. It has an outdoor kitchen/ grill and island-style bar."

DISTINCTIVE HOME XXV

The Owner – "The home was meant to be contemporary, but comfortable in Naples. It is taken from Low Country architecture, however all details are minimized to suggest vernacular architecture but in fact are contemporary. The home was designed to be able to show art, and that it does!"

"We used an all-white, monocramatic interior palette to display the homeowner's colorful and dramatic art."

DESCRIPTION / RESOURCES

BUILT	2009
TOTAL AREA	5,800 SF on 2 Levels
STYLE	Old Florida
ARCHITECT	Stofft & Cooney Architects - Naples, FL
BUILDER	BCB Homes - Naples, FL
INTERIOR DESIGN	Kevin Serba Interiors - Birmingham, MI
CABINETRY	AlliKristé Fine Cabinetry & Kitchen Design - Naples, FL
LANDSCAPING	Renfroe & Jackson, Inc. - Naples, FL
LANDSCAPE & POOL DESIGN	Architectural Land Design, Inc. - Naples, FL
RECOGNITION	*Home & Design* feature; Southern Home Sand Dollar Award - Naples, FL
PHOTOGRAPHY	Giovanni Photography & Glenn Hettinger, AIA

"I like that it is grand, yet intimate, highly designed, and yet warm and inviting. The floor plan is zoned so that it provides privacy for every area, yet affords large and gracious entertaining areas."

Architect – "Our client wanted a very modern home to display his modern art. But he was concerned about the resale value if the home was not built in a more traditional style. Our solution was to design a traditional exterior in an Old Florida vernacular, and to include traditional coffered ceilings. We also took advantage of the breathtaking bay views."

DISTINCTIVE HOME XXVI

Owners – "Our home is a warm, friendly and fun home to share with family and friends. The color and texture of our woods, paint colors and fabrics are soothing. The doors all open fully and really bring the outside in. It takes full advantage of the water views and activities. Our open airy landscaping even blends into the water."

Interior Designer – "I was lucky enough to have not only great clients but a great building team. Our objective was to use lots of natural light and make the space very inviting for not only the family but guests. The transition from outside to inside is seamless, which completed the package for their enjoyment."

DESCRIPTION / RESOURCES		
BUILT	2005	
TOTAL AREA	9,000 SF on 2 Levels	
STYLE	Caribbean Island Estate	
HOME DESIGN	The Sater Group, Inc. - Bonita Springs, FL	
BUILDER	Kurtz Homes Naples - Naples, FL	
INTERIOR DESIGN	Nancy H. Ruzicka Interiors - Mission Hills, KS	
CABINETRY	C&C WoodWorking, LLC - Naples, FL (formerly Baker's Cabinets)	
LANDSCAPE & POOL DESIGN	The Late Russell P. Bencaz - Naples, FL	
DOCKS	Garland & Garland Marine Construction - Naples, FL	
WINDOWS	Andersen Windows & NanaWall System	
RECOGNITION	Dream Homes Florida (cover) Sater's 30 Luxury Estate Homes	
PHOTOGRAPHY	CJ Walker Photography & Glenn Hettinger, AIA	

Builder - "Due to the unstable soils, we utilized concrete pilings to support the home. The owners were very involved in the selections and design of the home."

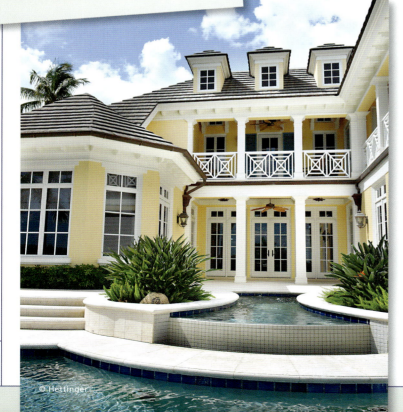

"The wood trusses were painted green to match some in the Port Royal Club. We used copper downspouts with little palm trees on them. Flat concrete tiles were used on the roof embossed with mitered-hip tiles."

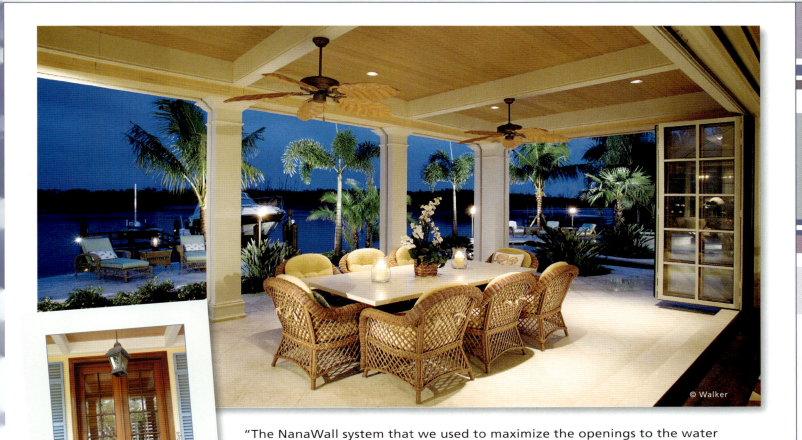

"The NanaWall system that we used to maximize the openings to the water features were metal to meet hurricane wind loads, but we had them faux painted to match the stain on the wood windows. I even helped the client to place sea shells that she had collected into the outdoor fireplace."

DISTINCTIVE HOME XXVII

Architect – "Because of the challenging shape of the site that is very narrow at the road side and wider at the bayside, a vertical character to the façade could be achieved. Charleston low country design as well as island plantation architecture served to inspire.

The formality and symmetry of the main body, which is taller than wide, creates a striking entry element that fits well among larger footprints in the neighborhood. This home has a monumental presence on approach but is cozy and extremely livable when passing through the front door."

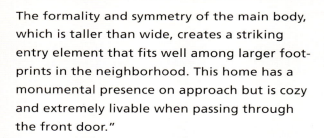

left: "Unusual disappearing privacy gate."

DESCRIPTION / RESOURCES		
BUILT	2009	
TOTAL AREA	6,500 SF on 2.5 Levels	
STYLE	Island & Low Country Plantation	
ARCHITECT	Harrell & Company Architects - Naples, FL	
BUILDER	BCB Homes - Naples, FL	
INTERIOR DESIGN	Interiors by previous owner	
LANDSCAPE & POOLS DESIGN	Architectural Land Design Inc. - Naples, FL	
PHOTOGRAPHY	Lori Hamilton Photography & Glenn Hettinger, AIA	

"The interior is 'open plan' — but it discreetly maintains enough room definition to suggest it could have been built a century ago. This is critical for unification of exterior and interior architecture which is always my concern when historical reference is the basis for the design."

DISTINCTIVE HOME XXVIII

"Piccola Villaggio"

Owners – "The entire team brought together talent, skills, and a passion for excellence that is evident in the final product! The result is beyond my wildest dreams but in line with my expectations for what a home should be!"

Architect – "'***Rustic***' this was the word architect Ron Olbekson received from his client. With further discussion it became clear this did not mean run-of-the-mill Mediterranean. Rustic meant, an ancient Northern Italy environment, almost Medieval."

BUILT	2014	
TOTAL AREA	16,800 SF on 2 Levels	
STYLE	Tuscan Estate	
ARCHITECT	Ocean Architecture, Inc. - Ft. Myers, FL	
BUILDER	The Williams Group, Inc. - Naples, FL	
INTERIOR DESIGN	SMC Design - Bay Village, OH	
LANDSCAPE & POOL DESIGN	Neumann Landscape Architecture & Architectural Land Design, Inc. - Naples, FL	
WINDOWS	Andersen Architectural Collection - Eagle Series - Naples, FL	
AUTOMATION	Lutron Home Automation - Naples, FL	
PHOTOGRAPHY	Jim Freeman Photographer & Dave Ross Photographer & Glenn Hettinger, AIA	

Architect – "He called his vision 'the complex' because of the number of pieces that comprised the estate: Building, Pools, Parks, Loggia etc… soon it started to look like a little village thus "Piccola Villaggio" was formed. Upon entering the property you experience the foliage of Italy."

"The Rotunda has heavy wooden entry gates and three-foot thick walls. Passing through you are immediately overwhelmed with beautiful vistas across the courtyard, the pool and wide waterway."

"One side of the home is The Master's House with generous space… the Noble Guest House with its homey guest room across the courtyard balances the overall complex. The outdoor trellis picnic area with fireplace and exotic plantings separate the Guest House from the Loggia. The Loggia creates a poolside getaway for cooking, relaxing and enjoying the view."

Interior Designer – "My challenge was to create a 300 year old Tuscan Village in the Southwest Florida tropics. Once my interior inspirations began to develop my love for history, art and nature took over."

"Many trips throughout Europe helped deliver the authentic elegance of this home. Attention to detail, and caring for the way my clients live goes into creating a warm distinctive home."

DISTINCTIVE HOME XXIX

THE VINCENT & NANCY BORELLI HOME

Owners – "When we sat down to design this home we wanted to create a home where you could feel comfortable, entertain, and accommodate plenty of bedrooms for guests. We created larger than average bedrooms and oversized the closets. We wanted everyone to be comfortable no matter where in the house they may be. We try to be different than every house on the block and to stand out to create a reaction as you drive by."

DESCRIPTION / RESOURCES		
BUILT	2013
TOTAL AREA	9,612 SF on 2 Levels
STYLE	Classical Florida Revival
ARCHITECT	Stofft Cooney Architects - Naples, FL
BUILDER	Borelli Construction of Naples - Naples, FL
INTERIOR DECOR	Nancy Borelli - Naples, FL
CABINETRY	CABNU Cabinets, Inc. - Naples, FL
LANDSCAPE & POOL DESIGN	Sunset Landscaping - Naples, FL
WINDOWS	Andersen Windows 400 Series, Storm Watch - Naples, FL
AUTOMATION	Superior Electric of Naples, Inc. - Naples, FL
PHOTOGRAPHY	Giovanni Photography & Glenn Hettinger, AIA

Architect – "This is a great example of golf course community living at its finest. It has great golf course views that can be enjoyed with casual outdoor living. The Borelli's broke away from the heavy Mediterranean homes so prevalent in Naples and started a trend of a more contemporary look. We mixed tropical design with a contemporary flair. And then they made it very eclectic in the detailing which more and more people are copying. The monumental stair is certainly a focal point in the understated but impressive entryway."

Builder – "Building our personal home is always one of our favorite projects. We often experiment in new designs and styles. The curved glass staircase was a new thing for us and it turned the foyer into a focal point of the home. The exterior of our home is simple refined elegance. The stone and white washed wood accents offset the brown roof tile and driveway to make the house really show from the street. We optimized the lake view on the rear of the home with second floor balconies and by raising up the home and creating a raised lawn on the back of the pool."

Interior Decor – "It has always been a passion of mine to decorate our personal homes. We used a transitional style in this house. We used modern cabinets offset with more subtle furnishings. White is a main theme in the design with hints of color in the wood accents and fabrics. I spent a year selecting items for our home from many sources. Selecting the artwork is one of my favorite parts of designing a home and this house has many great spaces for artwork."

DISTINCTIVE HOME XXX

"Mermaid Memories"

Owners – "Our desire was to create an even more open feel in our great room by adding French doors, using lighter and brighter tones, and moving away from traditional design by adding a nautical motif and modern elements. We also needed to create more space for our growing family so a second floor was necessary. But it was important to us to keep the house style in harmony with our original 2006 design."

left: The play agenda spills out into the yard with the kids playhouse and swing, setting the tone.

below: "A 'Cheaphuly' chandelier mimics the Chihuly glass art pieces."

DESCRIPTION / RESOURCES		
BUILT	2006 and 2014 Major Remodel	
TOTAL AREA	2,600 SF on 2 Levels	
STYLE	Whimsical Arts & Crafts	
BUILDER	Safety Harbor Builders - Boca Grande, FL	
HOME DESIGN	Energy Smart Home Design, LLC - Fort Myers, FL	
INTERIOR DESIGN	Jena Benner - Homeowner	
CABINETRY	AlliKristé Fine Cabinety & Kitchen Design - Naples, FL	
LANDSCAPE MANAGEMENT	Southern Gulf-West - Naples, FL	
WINDOWS	Andersen Windows & Doors & Marvin Windows and Doors	
AUTOMATION	Crestron Electronics, Inc. - Naples, FL	
PHOTOGRAPHY	Jena Benner & Glenn Hettinger, AIA	

AFTER

BEFORE

Home Designer - Dave Jenkins - "This second-story addition to an already 'picture perfect' cottage home presented many challenges. The main pressure was between adding the many 'must haves' on the client list, but at the same time not overwhelming the first floor. Working with David Benner of Safety Harbor Builders was key in the design and construction process – keeping critical aesthetic elements in check, while maximizing every square inch of space."

"The owners were actively involved in the process and very detail oriented. The result was adding 924 SF to the 1,617 SF home, with the addition of a bonus/game room, guest suite, powder bath, and laundry room. Most importantly — the second floor is in complete harmony with the first, and looks like it was always meant to be that way."

above: "This is a bold and heavenly playroom for the sweetheart of the house, complete with 'playhouse' with a Dutch door."

Interior Designer — "The artistic objective was to recreate the feel of the vintage Ralph Lauren store in East Hampton; the historic cottages in Sag Harbor, NY; and a neighborhood in my hometown of Ocean City, NJ called 'The Gardens.'"

DISTINCTIVE HOME XXXI

Architect – "This estate compound inside of a golf course community started as one home on one lot. I knew the clients for twelve years and when they discovered that I had designed it they bought the one home and the lot next door for gardens and a guest house. Christian Andrea then designed a water feature in the middle that did a beautiful job of tying it all together. Borelli masterfully built it, and now we're designing another quite different home for the same homeowners in South Carolina."

Interior Designer – "This was the kind of creative collaboration that you dream about with this great design team and amazing visionary clients. Our mix of textures and materials created unique and highly detailed spaces, a hallmark of our work."

BUILT	2010
TOTAL AREA	10,400 SF on 2 Levels
STYLE	Tropical West Indies
ARCHITECT	Stofft Cooney Architects - Naples, FL
BUILDER	Borelli Construction of Naples - Naples, FL
INTERIOR DESIGN	Montanna & Associates - Naples, FL
CABINETRY	SOHO Kitchens & Design, Inc. - Naples, FL
LANDSCAPE & POOL DESIGN	Architectural Land Design, Inc. - Naples, FL
WINDOWS	Andersen Windows 400 Series, Storm Watch - Naples, FL
AUTOMATION	Superior Electric of Naples - Naples, FL
RECOGNITION	*Gulf Shore Life* - At Home Magazine Cover
PHOTOGRAPHY	Lori Hamilton Photography & Christian Andrea

Builder – "When we started this home we set out to create a home different from the normal Naples home. The West Indies styling was different than anything else in the neighborhood at the time."

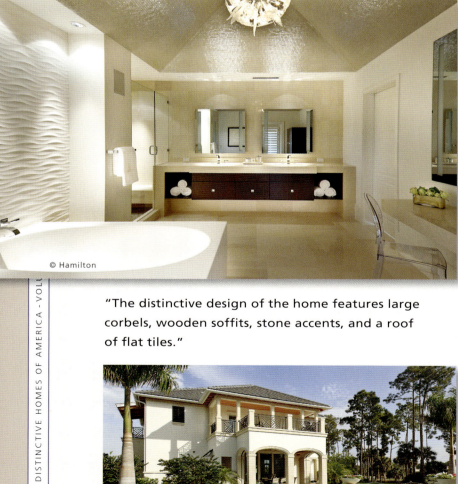

"The distinctive design of the home features large corbels, wooden soffits, stone accents, and a roof of flat tiles."

"Later, when we reimagined the design of the home and guest house for the owners, we used our same signature styling which the homeowners loved. The overall project ended up with a beautiful product everyone was happy with."

DISTINCTIVE HOME XXXII

Architect/ Builder – "The formal symmetry of the home and hardscape evolved in response to the owner's program and the grand scale requirements. The finishes and architectural details humanized the scale."

BUILT	2009
TOTAL AREA	10,000 SF on 3 Levels
STYLE	Formal Mediterranean
ARCHITECT	Eugene E. Martin, AIA, - Naples, FL
BUILDER	Martin Custom Homes, Inc. - Naples, FL
INTERIOR DESIGN	Janie Petkus Design - Hinsdale, IL
CABINETRY	Wood-mode Fine Custom Cabinetry - Naples, FL
LANDSCAPE ARCHITECT	Architectural Land Design, Inc. - Naples, FL
POOL DESIGN	Martin Custom Homes, Inc. - Naples, FL
STONE SUPPLIER	Limestone Dimensions, Inc. - Naples, FL
STONE DESIGN & INSTALLATION	Stonery, Inc. - Naples, FL
WINDOWS	HURD Windows & Doors - Medford, WI
AUTOMATION	Syn-Er-Gy Custom Technology Solutions - Naples, FL
PHOTOGRAPHY	Craig Hildebrand Photography & Glenn Hettinger, AIA

"Due to the required flood elevation, 14' above grade, the house was elevated above a 10,000 SF garage and storage area. The grand entry stair, with multiple landings, was designed to mitigate the elevated look of a 'stilt structure.'"

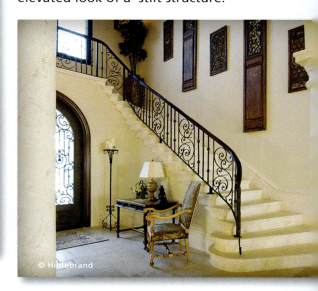

"All rooms, with the exception of the theater and bunk room, were positioned with views of the Gulf. An elevated pool terrace with a double sided negative edge spa was designed between twin lanais to capture the magnificent sunset views."

DISTINCTIVE HOME XXXIII

"La Playa"

Architect – "The client is in our industry and knew what he wanted, but also knew he wasn't an architect. He was very involved with every decision in what was supposed to be their life long home. Not the pool area, but the Gulf was the focal point of the design."

"There is so much different about this home than even in the typical high-end Naples homes. The windows and doors are Tischler und Sohn, one of the best in the world. The roof is formed concrete and if any home is left after a horrendous hurricane it will be this one. And, the home and the grounds are always impeccably maintained."

BUILT	2011
TOTAL AREA	8,476 SF + 1,279 SF Guest House
STYLE	Old Florida with Nantucket Flair
ARCHITECT	Stofft Cooney Architects - Naples, FL
BUILDER	BCB Homes - Naples, FL
INTERIOR DESIGN	Collins & DuPont Interior Design - Naples, FL
CABINETRY	Busby Cabinets - Naples, FL
LANDSCAPE ARCHITECT	Architectural Land Design, Inc. - Naples, FL
WINDOWS	Tischler und Sohn - Delray Beach, FL
RECOGNITION	*Home & Design* Magazine 2014
PHOTOGRAPHY	Lori Hamilton Photography

Builder - "The home was more complex because of the concrete roof system. Therefore we brought in specialists from the East Coast of Florida to assist us with the construction. This roof system will outperform any wood truss system, and can resist 300 mph sustained winds."

Builder - "Other benefits of the concrete roof system consist of thermal protection, fire protection, and termite protection. It is also more energy efficient than a typical wood truss system. The home was designed to be incredibly safe for the family with its concrete block walls from ground floor to top floor, with its concrete roof system, and with the generator to power the entire house."

left: The quaint, but spacious kitchen for the detached guest house above.

DISTINCTIVE HOME XXXIV

"Lookout"

Owners – "Naturally we love the long bay views and the 'extreme horizontal living' and casual feeling of just being here. We put casual country French earmarks all around to make our home look like a home that has been in the family for decades."

BUILT	2006
TOTAL AREA	9,760 SF on 2 Levels
STYLE	French Country Estate
HOME DESIGN	McHarris Planning & Design - Naples, FL
BUILDER	Harwick Homes - Bonita Springs, FL
INTERIOR DESIGN	Collins & DuPont Design Group - Naples, FL
CABINETRY	Bobby Benz - Naples, FL
LANDSCAPE & POOL DESIGN	The Late Russell P. Bencaz
WINDOWS	Andersen Windows & Doors
AUTOMATION	AVL Pro - Naples, FL
DOCKS	Naples Dock & Marine Services, Inc. - Naples, FL
RECOGNITION	Garden Club Tour & Naples Dailey News article; Ralph Lauren Home Party by Veranda
PHOTOGRAPHY	Naples Kenny & Glenn Hettinger, AIA

left: What a classic launch — to go out for a little jaunt around the bay.

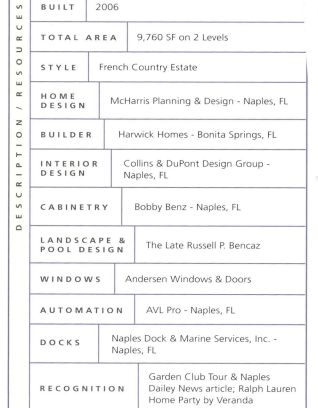

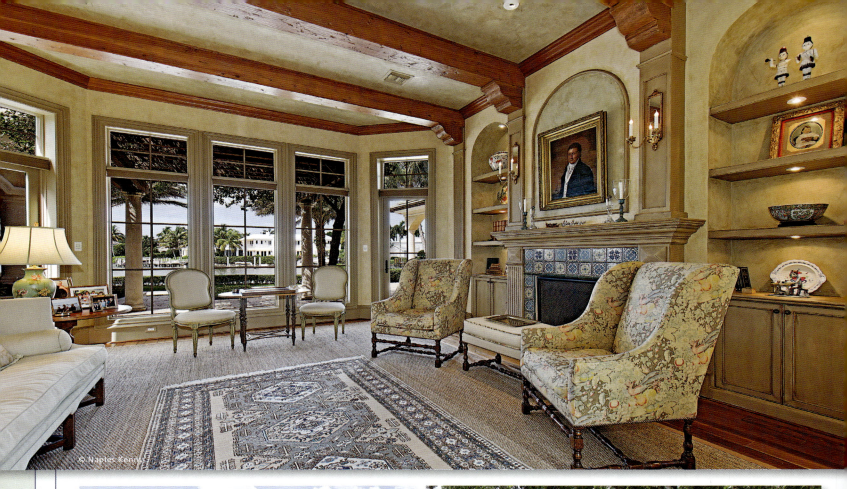

Architect – "Difficult sites create fantastic opportunities and this home proves just that. The lot is pie shaped and extremely tight at the front of the home and then opens up at the back to spectacular views of the long bay. Our task was to exploit these opportunities to the maximum while creating a classic and beautiful home for the owners. And that's just what we did."

Interior Designer – "This home was an inspired by homes in Provence, France. Almost all interior walls were faux painted to create the feeling of a gently aged country home. We also faux painted the entire exterior, including the shutters. The flooring is all rustic stone or walnut wood with an aged patina. Because most of our homes have been in the Northeast, the home is really a hodgepodge of things we have loved in previous homes added to the mix."

Builder – "This home created a unique opportunity for creativity due to the unusual lot location and size. Incorporating a French flare on a new home in South Florida and making it look as though it has been around for generations was a challenge that we embraced."

DISTINCTIVE HOMES OF AMERICA - VOLUME III - NAPLES, FLORIDA   XXXIV   141

DISTINCTIVE HOME XXXV

"The Four Treasures"

Architect – "This home occupies a 'long water view' site in close proximity to the attractive and quaint neighborhood church. The signature 'starburst' clerestory on the chapel building was incorporated into the symmetrical entry façade of the home in homage. The formality of the entry suggests Georgian influence but gives way to a more casual and playful feel on the water side façade. Brick elements were common to period architecture of the day but are not often seen in current transitional designs."

"The main entrance opens to the grand marble-lined foyer with circular stairs and spectacular water view just beyond the great room."

DESCRIPTION / RESOURCES		
BUILT	2005	
TOTAL AREA	11,200 SF on 2 Levels	
STYLE	Geogian Island	
ARCHITECT	Harrell & Company Architects - Naples, FL	
BUILDER	Borelli Construction of Naples - Naples, FL	
INTERIOR DESIGN	Harrell & Company together with the Owners- Naples, FL	
CABINETRY	Custom site built - Naples, FL	
LANDSCAPE & POOL DESIGN	The Late Russell P. Bencaz - Naples, FL	
WINDOWS	MQ Windows of Europe & The Americas - Dania, FL	
PHOTOGRAPHY	Lori Hamilton Photography & Glenn Hettinger, AIA	

"A large serving bar and seating areas around a large flat screen television are perfect for daytime fun. The patio is transformed at night with lighted arched columns, a fountain fire feature and custom tiki torches at the homes waterfront edge."

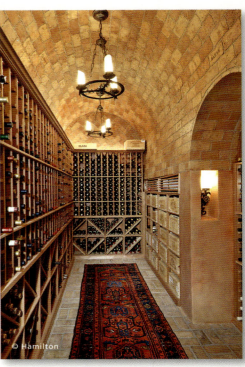

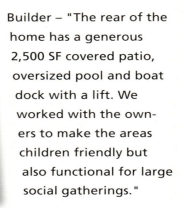

Builder – "The rear of the home has a generous 2,500 SF covered patio, oversized pool and boat dock with a lift. We worked with the owners to make the areas children friendly but also functional for large social gatherings."

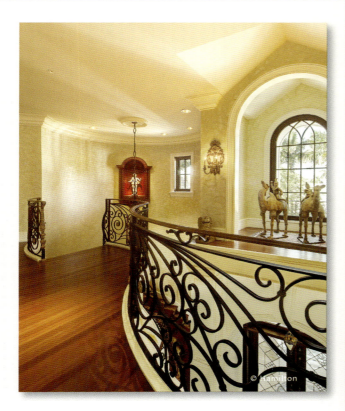

Architect – "Brick detailing was incorporated to create warmth and recall historical island architecture which perfectly complements the owner's love of art and antiques."

DISTINCTIVE HOME XXXVI

"Winsome"

Owners – "All of our design goals were achieved and we just love our Naples home."

Interior Designer – "One of the design goals for the home was to keep the color palette neutral so that the owners' personal collection of the artwork (landscapes and seascapes in gilt wood frames) would give each room a pop of color."

DESCRIPTION / RESOURCES	
BUILT	2004
TOTAL AREA	9,500 SF on 2 Levels
STYLE	British West Indies
ARCHITECT	Harrell & Co. Architects - Naples, FL
BUILDER	Newbury North Associates - Naples, FL
INTERIOR DESIGN	Lily's Interior Design - Naples, FL
CABINETRY	Newbury Millwork - Naples, FL
LANDSCAPE DESIGN	The Late Russell Bancaz - Naples, FL
POOL DESIGN	Nassau Pools Construction, Inc. - Naples, FL
WINDOWS	MQ Windows of Europe & The Americas - Dania, FL
PHOTOGRAPHY	CJ Walker Photography & Glenn Hettinger, AIA

right: "Both interior and exterior ceilings are masterfully crafted with reclaimed tidewater cypress."

"Because of the neutral color palette, textures, such as silk, suede, linen, wool and cotton were selected for the soft furnishings throughout the home, as well, as natural stone floors, warm woods for the furniture and Library paneling, brass lighting fixtures and hardware."

"The home is carefully sited to capture long water views down Treasure Cove. Extremely simple, but refined stone detailing in combination with classic shutters backdrops the simple formality of turf and box hedges to recall the most classic buildings on the island of Bermuda."

Architect – "This home is situated on one of the largest contiguous bay sites in Naples. The client desired to create an extremely understated residence that did not destroy the open feel provided by the expansive property. We elected to create a mostly one story design, not common in the neighborhood, with a separate guest house unified by a rhythmic elliptical arched loggia."

"Each stage of the interior decorating was successfully achieved with the owner's keen eye for detail, level of confidence and decisiveness which made the project a joy for me."

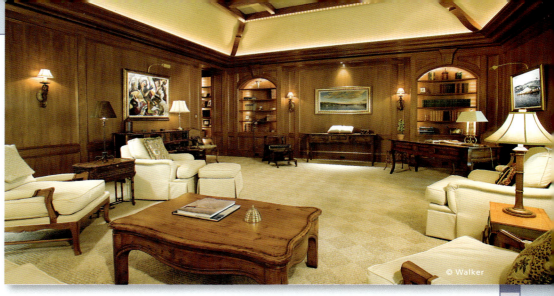

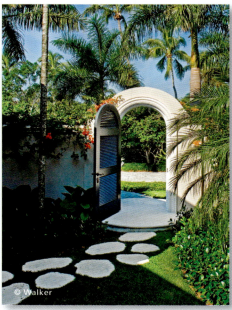

Builder – "I had the pleasure of working with my clients from the onset when they were searching for the right estate setting for their new home. Working throughout the construction project was an enjoyable experience because they had a discerning eye for detail and a great appreciation for craftsmanship."

"Great care was taken with various elements of the millwork, cabinetry, wood finishes, iron work and stone work. Most of the cabinetry was built by Newbury North's millwork shop. But, we also used trusted artisans from out of state and out of the country for various details including the butternut library, architectural plaster and iron work."

FOUR BAREFOOT BEACH HOMES

DISTINCTIVE HOME XXXVII

THE GILLETTE HOME
"Barefoot Beach"

Owners – "We like that we have such a large home with spacious rooms and a lot of natural light on a small footprint."

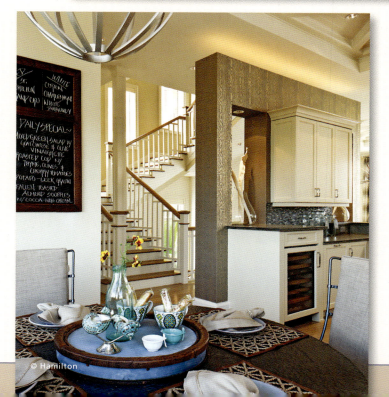

DESCRIPTION / RESOURCES		
BUILT	2013	
TOTAL AREA	4,389 SF to 4,770 SF in 4-Stories	
STYLE	West Indies to Transitional Contemporary	
ARCHITECT	Kukk Architecture & Design, P.A. - Naples, FL	
BUILDER	Potter Homes, Inc. - Naples, FL	
INTERIOR DESIGN	Collins & DuPont Interior Design - Naples, FL	
LANDSCAPE ARCHITECTURE	Architectural Land Design - Naples, FL	
WINDOWS	Andersen Windows & Doors	
RECOGNITION	*Home & Design* magazine	
PHOTOGRAPHY	Lori Hamilton Photography & Glenn Hettinger, AIA	

"We have the convenience of an attached four-car garage and an elevator to traverse our four stories. We also have two master suites, one with a private observation deck and luxurious finishes throughout."

DISTINCTIVE HOME XXXVIII

THE WINDOVER HOME I
"Barefoot Beach"

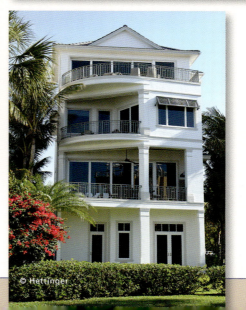

"No repetitive design was mandated by the community guidelines and the developer desired to create a distinctive street scape."

Architect – "It is not very often that a design team is given the challenge to create four individual homes side by side and on the same street."

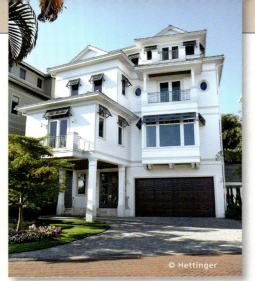

DISTINCTIVE HOME XXXIX

THE WINDOVER HOME II
"Barefoot Beach"

"This was the goal given to the team as it embarked on a design path to create four uniquely styled but harmonious beach side residences."

DISTINCTIVE HOME XL

"Barefoot Beach"

"The result is a grouping of four sibling homes, each with its own character and highlights, but coordinated to live complementary with each other. All the homes present a creative facade to the street from a traditional West Indies styling of one to the more transitional contemporary of another."

"Each home also shares a common beach garden set upon the shores of the Gulf of Mexico and will be home to owners as diverse as their designs."

BAREFOOT BEACH

DISTINCTIVE HOME XLI

THE RICHARD & CELESTE CALLAHAN HOME

Owners – "This home is big enough for all of our children and their families while still having enough privacy for everyone. We enjoy the unique design with the motor court, our koi pond, two decks and six-car garage."

Architect – "The oversized 'pie shaped' site created by a cul-de-sac location provided an opportunity to create nearly 180 degree views from many areas of the home."

DESCRIPTION / RESOURCES		
BUILT	1999	
TOTAL AREA	9,500 SF on 3 Levels	
STYLE	Colonial Plantation	
ARCHITECT	Harrell & Company Architects - Naples, FL	
BUILDER	BCB Homes - Naples, FL	
INTERIOR DESIGN	Romanza Interior Design - Naples, FL	
PHOTOGRAPHY	Glenn Hettinger, AIA	

"In order to maximize the views, the home fans out along the waterside building limit. Each main room is afforded the maximum amount of glass, usually on two different walls, creating a panorama from each room. The 'entry tower' at street side with wrap around balcony recalls a Caribbean lighthouse photograph which was the design inspiration."

Interior Designer - "Traditional fabrics and textures were interwoven with more modern accessories, blending the old and the new for a fresh, Florida 'transitional' atmosphere. The detailed patterns and textures are combined with bisque tones in the Turkish Travertine flooring to create a warm and inviting space for living."

above:
Henry guards the master bath.

DISTINCTIVE HOME XLII

THE DENNIS & LIZ HANSCH HOME
"Montelena"

Architects – "BCB and our firm were confident that we could create a new innovative home that would sell. We used solid floor to ceiling glass on the front and the rear of the home to let in tons of natural light. The use of split-faced stone added a contemporary touch as well as the use of interior stone walls."

Builder – "In addition to being a beautiful home, this home is the first single family residence to be certified by LEED® in Southwest Florida! One of the challenges in 'going Green' was the size of the home. The larger the home, in relation to the number of bedrooms, the more difficult it becomes to be certified as a 'Green' residence."

DESCRIPTION / RESOURCES		
BUILT	2010	
TOTAL AREA	5,300 SF on 1 Level	
STYLE	New Age Mediterranean Revival	
ARCHITECT	Stofft Cooney Architects - Naples, FL	
BUILDER	BCB Homes - Naples, FL	
INTERIOR DESIGN	Godfrey Design Consultants - Naples, FL	
CABINETRY	Tradewind Designs, Inc. - Naples, FL	
LANDSCAPE ARCHITECT	Outside Productions, Inc. - Naples, FL	
WINDOWS	Andersen 400 Series, Storm Watch - Naples, FL	
AUTOMATION	Criteria of Naples - Naples, FL	
LEED CONSULTANTS	E3 Building Sciences - Bonita Springs, FL	
RECOGNITION	The first single family residence to be certified LEED® in SW FL; *Gulfshore Life* Mag. April 2010; Several Sand Dollar Awards	
PHOTOGRAPHY	Lori Hamilton Photography & Glenn Hettinger, AIA	

"Some 'Green' attributes are concrete block wall systems, temporary air conditioning, and Icynene insulation. The concrete block exterior walls require minimal maintenance and cannot be damaged by water; in turn, they do not promote mold growth which helps maintain a healthy, safe living environment Icynene insulation is sprayed throughout the entire residence which creates a continuous air barrier in the walls, ceilings, and floors, which effectively minimizes the intrusion of outdoor allergens and pollutants."

"The air conditioning and dehumidification systems are key components in establishing the Montelena as a 'Green' residence. While introducing a treated outdoor air into the home, the units provide fresh air to breathe and dilute indoor air pollutants. Due to the window-to-wall ratio in the home, the windows used were extremely important."

"Low-E windows were installed which deliver the ideal balance of solar control and high visibility. All kitchen and utility equipment are Energy Star® rated, and a Crestron home automation system was installed throughout to help control all of the daily energy consumption."

DISTINCTIVE HOME XLIII

THE GEORGE HASEOTES & KRISTEN WILLIAMS-HASEOTES HOME

"The Happy House"

Owners – "Every room opens unto a view of the atrium butterfly garden in the very center of our home. So there is life and sunshine at every turn. That's why the home is called by many '*The Happy House*.'"

Architect – "I was honored to work on updating the design of an Alfred W. French, III original design. We just had to remove a few walls to make the home blossom again with better traffic flow and the kind of visual openness that people now expect."

DESCRIPTION / RESOURCES		
BUILT	1991 Rehab: 2014	
TOTAL AREA	6,300 SF on 2 Levels	
STYLE	Bermuda Island	
REMODEL ARCHITECT	MHK Architecture & Planning - Naples, FL	
ORIGINAL ARCHITECT	Alfred W. French, III - Naples, FL	
BUILDER	Waterside Builders, Inc. - Naples, FL	
INTERIOR DESIGN	Kristen Williams - Naples, FL	
CABINETRY	Hyland Custom Cabinetry - Naples, FL	
LANDSCAPING	Sunnygrove Landscaping & Nursery, Inc. - Naples, FL	
INTERIOR & EXT. PLANTINGS	Mike & Jackie Malloy Naples Butterfly - Naples, FL	
WINDOWS	Andersen 400 Series, Storm Watch - Naples, FL	
RECOGNITION	*Home & Design* 2014 - Cover; Naples Garden Club Tour	
PHOTOGRAPHY	Giovanni Photography	

above: The distinctive sliding barn doors at the kitchen and dining room passageway were made from heavy English Elm slabs by Hyland Custom Cabinetry.

DISTINCTIVE HOME XLIV

THE KURTZ HOME

Owners – "We built this home to live in ourselves. We were the first home to be built in Mediterra without a barrel tile roof. Our children wanted some hidden doors to play hide-and-seek and we were happy to accommodated that. We also built two stairways with the back one going to the billiard room and theatre which seats 17 people."

left: A winding driveway fit for a castle... framed by stone columns and tall trees.

	BUILT	2001
	TOTAL AREA	7,850 SF on 2 Levels
	STYLE	Country French
DESCRIPTION / RESOURCES	ARCHITECT	Harrell & Company Architects - Naples, FL
	BUILDER	Kurtz Homes Naples - Naples, FL
	INTERIOR DESIGN	Calvin Lee Interiors - Naples, FL
	CABINETRY	Eric Baker - Naples, FL
	LANDSCAPE ARCHITECT	Windham Studio, Inc. - Bonita Springs, FL
	POOL DESIGN	Don's Quality Pools - Naples, FL
	PHOTOGRAPHY	CJ Walker Photography & Glenn Hettinger, AIA

"When we built the pool area we added a private one-bedroom cabana as a guest house. The hidden motor court with five car garages was all my thing."

DISTINCTIVE HOME XLV

"Home in the Sky"

The Owners – "Where else can you find beach access and deep water dockage, perfect east to west sun light, our total automation, security, serenity and an outdoor master shower. We love it all!"

DESCRIPTION / RESOURCES		
BUILT	2006; Remodeled 2013	
TOTAL AREA	7,400 SF on 2 Levels	
STYLE	French Caribbean Plantation	
ARCHITECT	Harrell & Company Architects - Naples, FL	
BUILDER	Hemmer Construction - Naples, FL	
INTERIOR DESIGN	Taylor & Taylor, Inc. - Miami Beach, FL	
CABINETRY	Wallace Woodworks Artisans Inc. - Naples, FL	
LANDSCAPE & POOL DESIGN	Windham Studio, Inc. - Naples, FL	
WINDOWS	Andersen 400 Series, Storm Watch - Naples, FL	
RECOGNITION	*Florida Architecture* - 79th Addition	
PHOTOGRAPHY	Naples Kenny Photography & Glenn Hettinger, AIA	

Architect – "Situated on the desirable but precarious strip of land between Gulf Beach and inland estuary, this property has to consider the possibility of water intrusion during a hurricane."

"French Caribbean influence, was infused utilizing multiple smaller buildings at different levels. Connections through the tree canopy, including a wood gazebo that hovers over a reflecting pond adjacent to the main entry, create a magical juxtaposition of 'man-made' structure and native Florida vegetation."

"Requirements to elevate the air conditioned living areas above the flood plain provided an opportunity to create a *'home in the sky.'* The owner desired understated formality, but not a traditional tree house or beach cottage on stilts."

"The area below the elevated home is transformed into the ultimate poolside living space. The home is at once an antique Caribbean plantation nestled in tropical forest and also an upscale island spa."

above: The beadboard ceiling gently cascades over the master bedroom, making a simple but elegant statement.

right: Soft curves and a sea-foam palette make this gorgeous master bath the author's favorite.

DISTINCTIVE HOME XLVI

Architect – "This home being an Italian Mediterranean called for more ornamentation than we would typically design. We concentrated on the details that included intricate moldings and stone work."

"Christian Andrea's landscape and hardscape designs are always a great compliment to our work and this home really exemplifies that. Every room has an outstanding view."

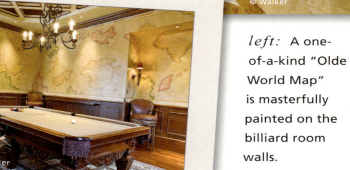

left: A one-of-a-kind "Olde World Map" is masterfully painted on the billiard room walls.

DESCRIPTION / RESOURCES		
BUILT	2004	
TOTAL AREA	Unlisted SF on 2 Levels	
STYLE	Italian Mediterranean Estate	
ARCHITECT	Stofft Cooney Architects - Naples, FL	
BUILDER	Kurtz Homes Naples - Naples, FL	
INTERIOR DESIGN	Montanna Design Associates - Naples, FL	
CABINETRY	Busby Cabinets - Naples, FL	
LANDSCAPE & POOL DESIGN	Architectural Land Design, Inc. - Naples, FL	
STONEWORK	Henthorne Precast - Naples, FL	
RECOGNITION	Host Home to the Wine Festival	
ELEVATOR	Taylor Elevators - Naples, FL	
PHOTOGRAPHY	CJ Walker Photography & Glenn Hettinger, AIA	

Interior Designer – "Our client wanted a timeless and comfortable home that incorporated collections from their trips to Europe. So, we complemented the homes' interior details with distinctive fabrics to create an elegant balance."

Builder – "What an incredible project, the marble and granite alone was sourced from six different places. The ornate stone work around the front entrance was cast in hand carved wooden molds by Dan Henthorne. There is a hidden door in the foyer and another fun item was the custom painting on the billiard room walls. The Master Suite is upstairs with a sitting area overlooking great views in all directions."

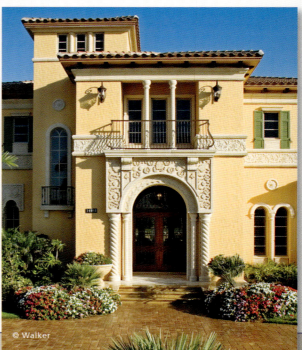

DISTINCTIVE HOME XLVII

THE TIM & CINDY HALLER HOME

DESCRIPTION / RESOURCES	BUILT	2011
	TOTAL AREA	5,200 SF on 2 Levels
	STYLE	French Country Estate
	HOME DESIGN	McHarris Planning & Design - Naples, FL
	INTERIOR DESIGN & CURATOR	Gordon L. Doane Residential Interiors - North Fort Myers, FL
	CABINETRY	Tradewind Designs, Inc. - Naples, FL
	LANDSCAPE & POOL DESIGN	Windham Studio, Inc. - Naples, FL
	WINDOWS	Andersen Windows - 400 Series, Storm Watch
	PHOTOGRAPHY	Windham Studio, Inc. & Glenn Hettinger, AIA

Owners – "We love all of our outdoor living areas, and we wanted to 'bring the outside in.' We accomplished that very well with the use of a lot of glass while maintaining an authentic historical French Country style."

Interior Designer – "The joy of helping Cindy and Tim create a distinctive Naples vacation home was one of the great pleasures of my career. I have always said that, 'A job is only as good as the clients.' The creation of their home was made easy by their wanting and willingness to appreciate the smallest and finest details that separate a warm, inviting beautiful home from just a house."

"Cindy had started the project with piles of photos of details taken in France of old fine residences. The fun was to translate her desire of the fine old world detail into their new Florida home. We created stone walls with the look of several centuries, and vaulted brick ceilings of French stables and country homes of the past. It all melded together to give their new home the character and authentic look of a 250 year old French country house. The jewel box of detail then needed the accessories to match. So we actually roamed and shopped Paris for the furnishings, linens and accessories needed to fill the new home."

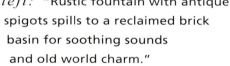

left: "Rustic fountain with antique spigots spills to a reclaimed brick basin for soothing sounds and old world charm."

Architect – "Every so often you get a chance to work with owners that have a strong sense of design as opposed to just copying something. These clients pushed our team's boundaries to create something truly unique. They had a clear sense of design, and knew what they wanted. Our job our course was to coordinate all of these concepts into a functioning work of art."

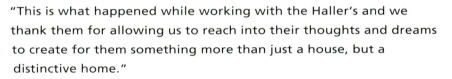

"This is what happened while working with the Haller's and we thank them for allowing us to reach into their thoughts and dreams to create for them something more than just a house, but a distinctive home."

left: "Our 'Carpe Diem' plaque over the fireplace memorializes Matthew, our son and Jessica's brother, whom we lost on April 12, 2007."

DISTINCTIVE HOME XLVIII

"Posada del Sol"

Owners – "We wanted a home with lots of brightness and happiness, and we wanted it to flow easily from the inside to the outside. We ended up with lots of distinctive design features which fill our home with joyfulness."

Architect – "The original home was a 1-story Florida/Bermuda style built in the 1950's. My client asked me to save the existing slab and to transform it into a Tuscan style design."

BUILT	1994
TOTAL AREA	7,530 SF + 1,900 SF Porches on 2 Levels
STYLE	Italian Whimsical Naples
ARCHITECT	Jerry DeGennaro, AIA Architect - Naples, FL
REMODEL BUILDER	Newbury North Associates, Inc. - Naples, FL
INTERIOR DESIGN	Owner - Naples, FL
SPECIALTY FURNISHINGS	MacKenzie Childs - Aurora, NY
LANDSCAPE ARCHITECT	The late Russell P. Bencaz - Naples, FL
WINDOWS	Pella Aluminum Clad Casement Windows - Pella, IA
PHOTOGRAPHY	Glenn Hettinger, AIA

"The 3,900 SF space, because of the client's wish list, had to double in size and acquire a second story. I have traveled the world several times, taking photos of details wherever I go. For this home expansion, I took a stated desire for a 'Mediterranean' style and introduced a number of European design elements."

"Loggias of the Lake Como area of Northern Italy, the teak front door of Malta design, and Palladian towers, resulted in a solution to practical problems. To connect the carriage house, I applied the loggias around the original structure to create an almost Monastery feeling."

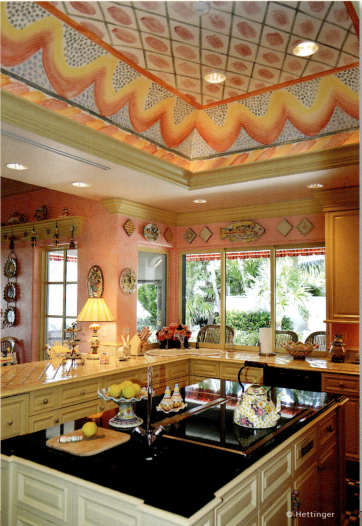

"With their Italian arches, they give shade and framed the views like picture frames. The Court Drive has an inviting effect with its curved pergola, defining the point of entry.

The house has a lot of authentic European elements. If you go back to the classics, you can't lose. I called it 'Palazzo-on-the-Gulf.'"

above: Bright and fun pieces from MacKenzie-Childs.

The home is brimming with an extensive MacKenzie-Childs whimsical collection of hand-crafted furniture and ceramics.

DISTINCTIVE HOME XLIX

THE SNYDER HOME

Owners – "With family being our main focus, we wanted a custom home that was warm and welcoming with an open, informal floor plan. We wanted plenty of room for our children and grandchildren to play, swim, fish, boat and sleep over."

"We selected this location so our family could walk or bike to all the local attractions - beach, restaurants and shopping. Fossilized white shells as mulch and 170 different plant species and trees surround our home and assist in the tropical aesthetic of the design. The way the design was executed from beginning to end left us with the perfect family home."

DESCRIPTION / RESOURCES		
BUILT	2013	
TOTAL AREA	5,814 SF on 3 Levels	
STYLE	Old Florida & Coastal Caribbean	
ARCHITECT	Weber Design Group, Inc. - Naples, FL	
BUILDER	Grand Bay Building & Development Corp. - Naples, FL	
INTERIOR DESIGN	Sandra Snyder - Naples, FL with Collins & Dupont Interior Design - Bonita Springs, FL	
CABINETRY	Xavier's Collection of Fine Cabinetry - Naples, FL	
LANDSCAPE DESIGN	EcoBotanic Designs, Inc. - Naples, FL	
POOL CONSTRUCTION	Serenity Pool & Spa - Bonita Springs, FL	
WINDOWS	Andersen Windows - 400 Series, Storm Watch - Naples, FL	
AUTOMATION	Lutron Lighting - Naples, FL	
RECOGNITION	Naples Home & Garden Tour 2015	
PHOTOGRAPHY	Giovanni Photography & Glenn Hettinger, AIA	

Architect – "This design is a blend of Old Florida and Coastal Caribbean, hosting a blend of materials. We used a tabby finish just above the grade, lap siding, bead board, tongue and groove ceiling materials both inside and out. We also used exterior shutters throughout the home adding both contrast and color. The home was designed to nestle in with a community of unique architecture.

It also brings back the character and coziness of the casual but sophisticated blend of indoor and outdoor living. It takes full advantage of the incredible coastal climate."

Builder - "The location of this Caribbean inspired home, with its view of the waterway, lends itself to the casual elegance the home owner desired. Much attention to detail was brought to the exterior, such as vertical boards that gracefully accentuate the subtle color variation from the clapboard. Classic Florida design includes, a widow's walk, eave brackets and spandrels that decorate the porches."

Interior Designer – "The palette was inspired by the Suzani Style hand knotted rug with vibrant turquoise and hot orchid on a chocolate ground. The design is bright, playful, with a touch of the exotic. The home is very family friendly with lots of cozy spots to hang out together."

DISTINCTIVE HOME L

"The Happy House"

Owners – "We wanted to maintain the Key West style and to maximize our views when we did our major renovation. We also kept a Florida style inside that is understated. Our home nicely accommodates our children and grandchildren. …We named our home 'The Happy House' because of all our visitors who tell us, *'being in this home just makes me feel happy.'*"

DESCRIPTION / RESOURCES		
BUILT	1985 + 2001 Major Renovation	
TOTAL AREA	14,300 SF on 2 Levels	
STYLE	Key West Victorian Estate	
ARCHITECT	Kukk Architecture & Design, P.A. - Naples, FL	
BUILDER	Carlson Harris General Contractors - Naples, FL	
INTERIOR DESIGN	Mary Ann Bindley - Naples, FL	
CABINETRY	AlliKriste Kitchens - Bob Ostrowski - Naples, FL	
LANDSCAPE & POOL DESIGN	The Late Russell Bancaz - Naples. FL	
WINDOWS	Marvin Windows & Doors	
RECOGNITION	*Magazine* Feature Dec. 2004	
PHOTOGRAPHY	Glenn Hettinger, AIA	

Architect – "This distinctive home commands a prominent position overlooking Gordon Pass, a landmark to the passing boat traffic. The design is a unique blend of traditional American, Key West and Victorian styles. We have collaborated with three different clients to perfect it, and each client has required new perspectives and requirements."

"In addition to the general renovations and maintenance, several key additions have been made over time including a second rear facade tower, a master suite addition, and the relocation of the swimming pool to yield the space for a new kitchen and family room. We are proud to have taken care of this beautiful home's lineage and to have added to her story and design."

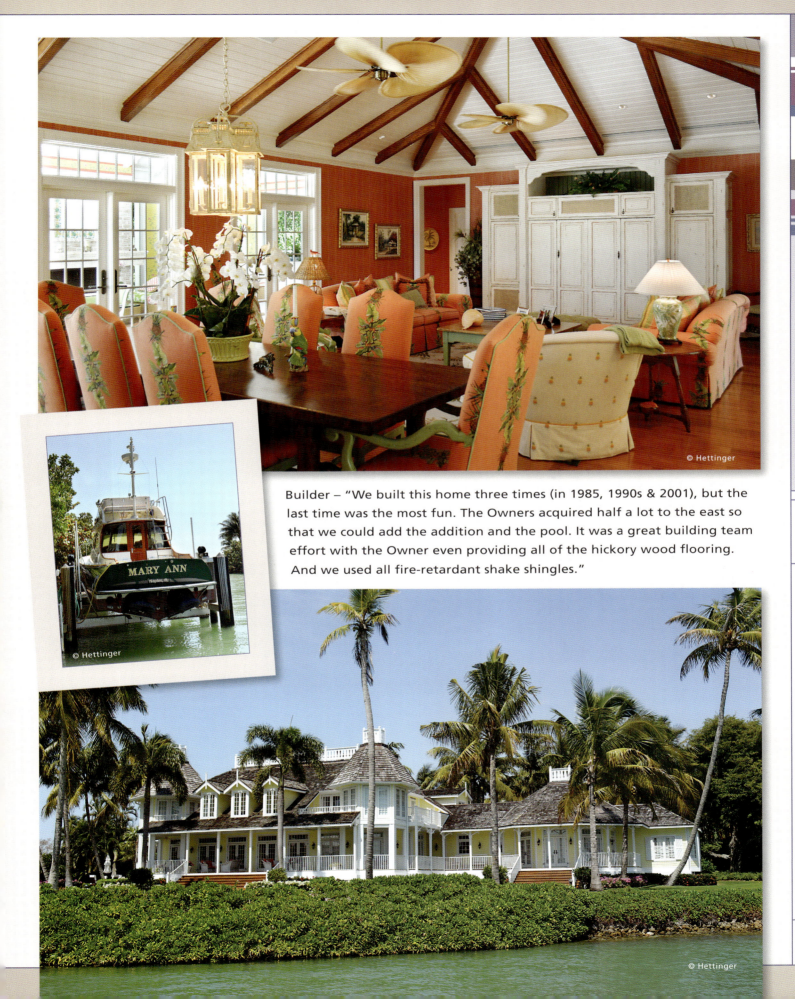

Builder – "We built this home three times (in 1985, 1990s & 2001), but the last time was the most fun. The Owners acquired half a lot to the east so that we could add the addition and the pool. It was a great building team effort with the Owner even providing all of the hickory wood flooring. And we used all fire-retardant shake shingles."

THIRTY-NINE MORE
HOMES OF DISTINCTION

There are too many distinctive homes from which to choose in Naples, Florida. So, the author thought that you would enjoy a glimpse of at least 39 more distinctive homes.

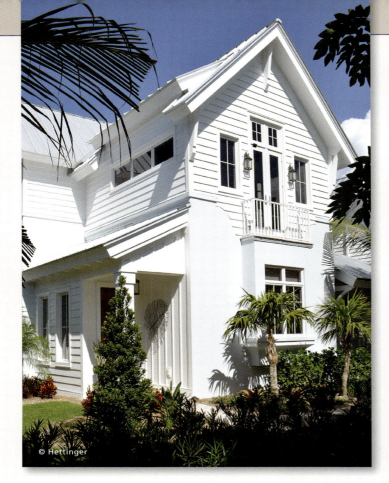

GREEN BUILDING INITIATIVES &
ENERGY-EFFICIENT DESIGN

All of the following items and more were implemented or at least considered by the owner and building team in this classically beautiful home. And almost all of these modern green aspects are hidden from sight. See pages 16-21. This list makes a great checklist for any building team to target when designing their new home.

Both the front and rear views of the home beautifully conceal its conservation elements.

USGBC LEED® for Homes: A national, third-party certification system for energy efficient, healthy, green homes.

LEED Consultant – *"There was an exceptional team that worked on this distinctive home. Because we were on the team early in the process it allowed us to earn a LEED Silver designation. But the real key to the success of this home was the "integration" of the disparate technologies such that they blended together seamlessly. The total house is significantly better than just the sum of the individual parts. The home is very efficient, comfortable and should enjoy a lower cost of ownership. The owners understood the complexity of a home this sophisticated and allowed the design / build team the time and money to do it right."* — John R. Kiefer, Ph.D., E3 Building Sciences

Architectural Design: The energy savings on this, and most any home, begins with the architectural design. Architect John Cooney designed this home with extensive overhangs and balconies which protect most all of the windows and doors from being attacked by direct sun light, while still allowing for magnificent views and reflected sun light into the interior.

High Performance Windows: The Weather Shield windows have a U-Factor .24, SHGC .27-. The 366 glass used throughout the windows and doors are impact rated for protection from exterior elements such as wind and debris, but they also contain the ultimate performing glass in terms of energy efficiency and solar heat gain.

Air Conditioning System: This home has a unique and customized Air Conditioning system. The Daikin A/C system is a smaller and smarter cooling system that is environmentally friendly. With traditional cooling systems, the only way to save energy and reduce power plant emissions is to turn the system off or to set it at a temperature that's not as comfortable as you might like it. With the Daikin cooling and heating system, there are multiple zones which let you set different temperatures for different rooms. This allows each room to control the temperature to the occupant's desires whether during the day or at night while sleeping. Not only does this make each room more comfortable, it also saves energy by eliminating overheating and overcooling.

Energy Star Appliances: Their efficient use of electricity while in operation, many of the appliances available today are approved through the Energy Star® program.

Geo-Thermal Pool Heating System: (ground source water) This system draws constant 70 degree well water from the stable ground into a heat exchange pool pump which in turn heats the pool water without the two sources even mingling. It is an excellent option as a pool heater because it can be used year round, is good for the environment, is extremely efficient, and is much less expensive to operate.

Savant Home Automation System: Savant's smart home system allows the homeowners to control and easily manage the amount of heating and cooling of their home, the pool's temperature and filtration, the lights, the audio/video system, and even Lutron controlled lights, electronic shades programmed on an astronomical clock and hurricane shutters.

Photovoltaic Whole House Water & Electric System: This system consists of 3 solar panels to heat the domestic hot water and 60 solar panels on the home's roof that generate electrical power by converting solar radiation directly into electricity. The PV system can produce up to 12.9 kilowatts of electricity which provides the family with enough electricity to power a very significant portion of the house. LED lighting was also used as well as insulation around all of the hot water pipes. A 100KW emergency generator provides the backup.

12.9 Kilowatt PV Solar Array System

FSC Certified Wood: Forest Stewardship Council (FSC) certified wood was used on the outdoor decking, the boat dock and for the front door. LEED for Homes has recognized the Forest Stewardship Council (FSC) as the world's only credible forest certification system.

Low Chemical Emission Materials: The low chemical emission paints were used throughout the home's walls, as well as in the cabinetry and shelving. The "Green Label Plus" certification is a voluntary testing program that establishes the highest standard for indoor air quality ever set by the carpet industry and all carpeting in the home has this certification.

Low Maintenance Materials: The use of synthetic exterior building materials, such as trim boards manufactured from PVC products, offer a long term solution to low maintenance by eliminating cracking, warping and rotting or moisture penetration. Synthetic decking materials made from recycled wood fiber, sawdust and plastic scrap provide a durable, moisture resistant alternative to wood deck products. Also, there is no pressed wood in the home.

All windows sun protected.

Use of Native Plants: The selection of native Florida trees and plants, which require less watering in the hot Florida summers and mild winter climate reduces the demand on irrigation usage.

Pervious Surfaces for the Driveway & Patios: Decorative granite pavers and sand-set stone were used in lieu of poured concrete, to allow percolation of water into the ground, reducing the water run-off into the storm water system and bay.

Bio-swale: Incorporated into the landscape design, and adjacent to the natural waterway, these bio-swales with river rock and drought-tollerant plantings are intended to capture the flow of surface water, thereby reducing the run-off of fertilizer and contaminated water into the storm water system and bay.

Sand-set pavers allow water to percolate into the storm drainage system and waterways.

BCB Project Manager - *"I invested additional time researching these 'green' products and learning about their features. I had a lot of fun working with the owners and the subcontractors for this home. There was a lot of sub involvement with their products and the homeowners were also very involved with the selections process and choosing what products went into their home. Everyone had a great time working together to build this amazing home, and now we have experience with a lot of new products that we can use in future homes BCB Homes builds."* — Chuck Rainey - BCB Homes' Vice President/Owner.

XXVII
TWENTY-SEVEN DISTINCTIVE MAILBOXES

What type of first impression does your mailbox make?
I believe that a distinctive (different in a positive way) home should also have a distinctive mailbox.
All of these mailboxes were found in Naples except for three of them.

Distinctive WINDOWS & DOORS

Andersen WINDOWS · DOORS

Southwest Florida
WINDOW & DOOR SELECTION

One item that probably telegraphs the quality of a distinctive home more than any other is the quality of the windows. It would be better to reduce the square feet of the home rather than to skimp on the quality of the windows and doors. They are a big part of the aesthetics of the exterior and interior of the home. They are an essential part of your energy savings and they frame the views of your magnificent lot and landscaping. They are also your first defense against hurricanes.

In Southwest Florida all windows and doors have to meet the strict building code design wind speeds and pressures. With that factor a given, the first real decision is about using aluminum or wood clad windows. Wood clad windows win out for their aesthetics but the cladding is all important. Vinyl wrapped sashes with the beauty of wood will not rot due to water damage which can be a big problem with some Aluminum clad type products. Aluminum also requires washing and rinsing every couple of months in order to maintain its warranty.

The glass in your windows has become a big issue with the energy codes constantly changing. The Andersen 'Circle of Excellence showroom' at Florida Wood Window and Door allows their clients to see firsthand how the different types of glass perform. They tell the whole story with full size displays, corner sections, hardware types and finishes and all the features available for each product.

No matter how good your windows and doors are they only perform as well as they are installed. A few years ago Florida Wood Window and Door established a division called Florida Install so when you came to them you could get a turnkey package. That's because it takes seasoned professionals to prepare the substrates, flash to windows and to join the exterior finish material (siding, brick, stone, stucco, etc.) to the window frames.

When people buy from FWWD they expect a level of service which they provide. Dan Shannon says, "I have customers that call from over ten years ago and if we did the job were going out at no charge to help fix the problem."

www.FWWDinc.com
www.AndersenWindows.com

Distinctive HOMES IN STONE

LIMESTONE DIMENSIONS

www.LimestoneDimensions.com

Where Architecture
BECOMES ART

There are distinctive homes and then there are distinctive stone homes.

For thousands of years, man has used colors, textures and the properties of stone to adorn structures of importance. It is no surprise that the seven wonders of the ancient and medieval world have one thing in common: stone. From the Great Pyramid of Giza to St. Paul's Cathedral in London and the Empire State Building in New York, limestone has been used throughout history in the creation of some of the world's most iconic structures.

Today, its unique qualities are used to provide both form, finish and durability to some of the finest homes in America. That's because while architectural styles may evolve over time, the strength, integrity and beauty of limestone has a permanence that transcends mere cultural preferences.

For stone to look beautiful it takes skilled hand-carvers with meticulous attention to detail in creating designs that complement the architectural style of the home. This quality is in evidence in the exterior cladding, staircases, fireplaces, bathrooms and pool decks which have been provided by Limestone Dimensions across the U.S. and beyond.

Based in Southwest Florida, they are renown for purveying the finest unique stone not readily available through local or international distribution channels. Key to their success is the ability to source high-grade, precision-carved, artisan-finished limestone from quarries across the world, including rich deposits in the Eastern Mediterranean, Eastern Europe and the Americas.

Distinctive NAPLES LIVING

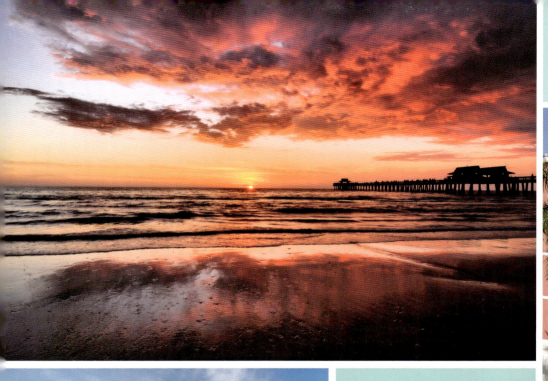

FIFTY DISTINCTIVE HOMES
DISTINCTIVE GUIDE

Some of the excellent Designers and Craftsman responsible for creating the 50 featured homes:

ARCHITECTS & HOME DESIGNERS

Stofft Cooney Architects
John Cooney -
Naples, FL - 239.262.7677

Randall Stofft -
Delray Bch, FL

D.Homes: #1, 4, 15, 19, 20, 25, 29, 31, 33, 42, 46

www.StofftCooney.com

MHK Architecture & Planning
Mathew H. Kragh
Naples, FL
239.331.7092

D.Homes: #7, 10, 16, 43

www.MHKap.com

Architecture Artistica, Inc.
Gerald J. Yurk, AIA
Naples, FL
239.222.4179

Ft. Myers, FL
D.Home: #3

www.ArchitectureArtisticaInc.com

Kukk Architecture & Design, P.A.
Jon Kukk, AIA
Naples, FL
239.263.9996

D.Homes: #2, 22, 37, 38, 39, 40, 50

www.KukkArchitecture.com

Weber Design Group, Inc.
Architecture & Planning
Bill & Kerry Weber
Naples, FL
239.594.9778

D.Homes: #17, 23, 49

www.WeberDesignGroup.com

R.G. Designs, Inc.
Rich Guzman, Designer
Bonita Springs, FL
239.949.2929

D.Home: #21

www.RGDesignsInc.com

McHarris Planning & Design
Joseph McHarris, Designer
Bonita Springs, FL
239.948.6688

D.Home: #34, 47

www.McHarris.com

Energy Smart Home Design, LLC
Dave Jenkins, Designer
Bonita Springs, FL
Ft. Myers, FL
239.218.3508

D.Home: #30

www.EnergySmartHomeDesign.com

INTERIOR DESIGN & DECORATING

Clive Daniel Home
Daniel Lubner
Naples, FL
239.261.4663
D.Home: #21

www.CliveDaniel.com

Montanna Design Associates
Sharon M. Gilkey, ASID
Winter Park, FL
407.339.7444
D.Homes: #20, 31, 46

www.Montanna.com

Tillie's Design Company & Assocites
Kenneth John Mabe, Allied ASID
Naples, FL
239.649.0333
D.Home: #18

www.TheTillieCompany.com

Gordon L. Doane Residential Interiors
Gordon L. Doane
N. Ft. Myers, FL
312.316.7910
D.Home: #47

GordonDoane@hotmail.com

Walters Design International
Jennifer Benner
Naples, FL
239.643.4611
D.Home: #30

jena.wdi@gmail.com

Jalan Jalan Collection, Inc.
Bruce Platt
Miami, FL
305.572.9998
D.Home: #3

www.JalanMiami.com

CK Interior Design, LLC
Cynthia K. Godoy, NCIDQ
Denver, CO
720.235.8206
D.Home: #1

www.CK-Interiors.com

Godfrey Design Consultants
Betsy & Lauri Godfrey
Winter Park, FL
239.267.8060
D.Home: #42

www.GodfreyDesignInc.com

WINDOWS & DOORS

Florida Wood Window & Door
Andersen Windows & Doors
Dan Shannon
Naples, FL
239.437.6166
D.Homes: #5, 6-12, 16, 17, 19, 20, 21, 26, 29, 30, 31, 34, 37-40, 42, 43, 45, 47, 49

www.AndersenWindows.com

Tischler und Sohn
Stamford, CT

Timothy Carpenter

800.282.9911

D.Home: #33

www.TischlerWindows.com

Solar Innovations, Inc.
Pine Grove, PA

570.915.1500

D.Home: #16

www.SolarInnovations.com

Hope's Windows, Inc.
Scott Farrell
Jamestown, NY

716.665.5124

D.Home: #2

www.HopesWindows.com

Weather Sheild Windows & Doors
Medford, WI

800.222.2995

D.Homes: #1, 4, 13, 14

www.WeatherShield.com

Hurd Windows & Doors
Medford, WI

800.433.4873

D.Homes: #22, 32

www.Hurd.com

CABINETRY

Tradewind Designs, Inc.
Todd E. Grooms
Naples, FL

239.354.4708

D.Homes: #3, 14, 22, 42, 47

www.TradewindNaples.com

STONEWORK

Limestone Dimensions, Inc.
Patrick J. McGirl
Naples, FL

239.253.2479 Cell

D.Homes: #13, 32

www.LimestoneDimensions.com

GENERAL CONTRACTORS

Kurtz Homes Naples
Randy Kurtz
Naples, FL
239.594.1501
D.Homes: #15, 19, 20, 26, 44, 46

www.KurtzHomes.com

BCB Homes
Joe Smallwood
Naples, FL
239.643.1004
D.Homes: #1, 14, 22, 25, 27, 33, 41, 42

www.BCBHomes.com

Grand Bay Building & Development Corp.
Naples, FL
239.643.3349
D.Homes: #5, 17, 23, 49

www.GrandBayDev.com

Old Naples Builders, Inc.
Pat Masters
Naples, FL
239.435.1909
D. Home: #3

www.OldNaplesBuilders.com

Borelli Construction of Naples
The Borelli Family
Naples, FL
239.263.7900
D.Homes: #29, 31, 35

www.BorelliConstructionOfNaples.com

Potter Homes, Inc.
Bill Potter & Tom Potter
Naples, FL
239.254.9319
D. Homes: #37, 38, 39, 40

www.PotterHomesInc.com

Newbury North Associates, Inc.
David S. Rogers
Naples, FL
239.434.2668
D. Homes: #36, 48

www.NewburyNorth.com

Naples ReDevelopment, Inc.
Adam Smith
Naples, FL - 239.331.7940
D.Homes: #6, 7, 8, 9, 10, 11, 12, 16

www.NaplesReDevelopment.com

Hemmer Construction, Inc.
Dan Hemmer
Naples, FL
239.649.8000
D. Homes: #45

www.HemmerConst.com

Thomas Riley Artisans' Guild
Matt Riley
Naples, FL
239.591.3203
D.Home: #2

www.ThomasRiley.net

REALTORS

John R. Wood Properties
Robyn Pfister Griffin, Realtor
Naples, FL
239.404.8222
D. Home: #5

www.RobynPGriffin.com

Keating & Associates
Real Estate Professionals
Thomas H. Hill, SRA
Naples, FL
813.810.7070
D.Home: #3

www.TomHillRealtor.com

Downing Frye Realty
Mary Catherine White, Realtor
Naples, FL
239.287.2818
D. Home: #43

www.NaplesLuxuryEstates.com

Premier Sotheby's International Realty
Karen Van Arsdale, Realtor
Naples, FL
239.403.4530
D.Home: #24

www.KarenVanArsdale.com

LANDSCAPE DESIGN

GardenBleu Landscape Architecture
Edward F. Westwood, Jr.
Naples, FL - 239.430.9995
D. Homes: #6, 7, 8, 9, 10 11, 12, 14

www.GardenBleu.com

Windham Studio, Inc.
Scott D. Windham, ASLA
Bonita Springs, FL
239.947.2396
D. Homes: #5, 19, 44, 47

www.WindhamStudio.com

POOL DESIGN

Serenity Pool & Spa
Wendy Carter
Bonita Springs, FL
239.597.7623
D. Homes: #5, 17, 48

www.SerenityPoolandSpa.com

Nassau Pools Construction, Inc.
Tommy Threlkeld
Naples, FL
239.206.1307
D.Home: #36

www.NassauPools.com

PHOTOGRAPHERS

Lori Hamilton Photography
Lori Hamilton
Naples, FL
239.595.5717

D.Homes: #1, 6-12, 14, 19, 20, 27, 31, 33, 35, 37-40, 42

www.LoriHamilton.com

Giovanni Photography
John Sciarrino
Naples, FL
239.263.2229

D.Home: #21, 22, 25, 29, 43, 49

www.GioPhoto.com

CJ Walker Photography
CJ Walker
West Palm Beach, FL
561.762.8451

D.Homes: #15, 26, 36, 44, 46

www.CJWalker.com

Naples Kenny Photography
Ken Siebenhar
Naples, FL
239.300.3609

D.Homes: #5, 23, 24, 34, 45

www.NaplesKenny.com

Keith Isaac Photography
Keith Isaac
Naples, FL
239.580.7194

D.Homes: #5, 17

www.KeithIsaac.com

Glenn D. Hettinger, AIA, ICAA
Ponte Vedra Beach, FL
904.881.8100

D.Homes: 45 of the 50 homes *(from partial to complete)*

www.DistinctiveHomesOfAmerica.com

Randall Perry Photography
Randall Perry
Naples, FL
239.261.0002
Cape Cod, MA
518.421.6834

www.RandallPerry.com

CHARITABLE FOUNDATION

Hope International
Chris Chancey
SE Region: Atlanta, GA
404.369.4566
HQ: Lancaster, PA
717.464.3220

A Hand Up, Not a Hand Out

www.HopeInternational.org

SMALL LOANS.
LASTING CHANGE.

Distinctive Homes of America supports HOPE International. It is a 'microfinance ministry' that empowers those in poverty with a hand up, not a handout. HOPE provides financial services and biblically based training that enable the poor to earn an income, initiate lasting change, and invest in what matters to them: from their homes, to health care and education for their children.

www.HopeInternational.org

Learn how you can Promote, Pray, Volunteer, Give or Go.

BOOKS
DISTINCTIVE HOMES OF AMERICA

If you wish to order additional copies of
"Distinctive Homes of America" books
please contact us directly.

www.DistinctiveHomesOfAmerica.com

glennhettinger@gmail.com

904.881.8100

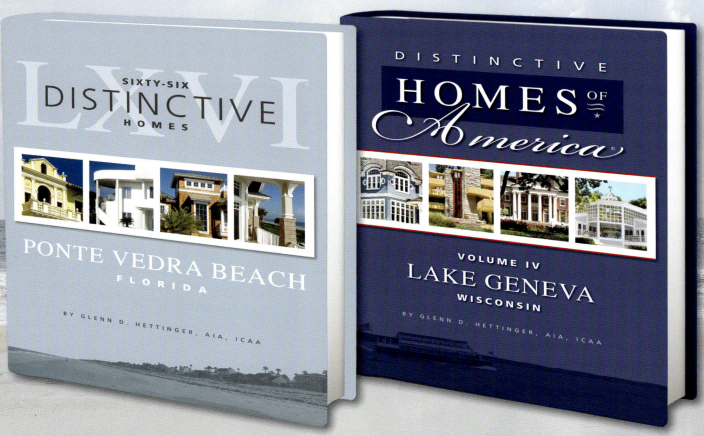

ABOUT THE AUTHOR

Glenn D. Hettinger, AIA, ICAA has designed, built and photographed homes for 40 years. As a practicing residential architect and photographer, Glenn recognizes the fine details that make a home distinctive – and is wonderfully adept at capturing them with his lens. Photographing gorgeous homes became his hobby and finally his passion.

He decided to be a 'home architect' in eighth grade. Soon after getting his architecture degree from Iowa State University, he started his own design / build home building company in Madison, WI. He is a principal in GDH Architects, P.A. in Ponte Vedra Beach, FL, where he and his wife raised their four sons.

His first book was '*Sixty-six Distinctive Homes of Ponte Vedra Beach, Florida.*' After its success, Glenn created the '*Distinctive Homes of America*' book series to celebrate and encourage the continuation of American design and craftsmanship of distinctive homes everywhere. His goal is that his books will be a blessing and inspiration to many.

If you wish to order additional copies of any of Glenn's series of books for friends, relatives or business associates, you may email or phone us directly. Please let us know if you are purchasing this book as a gift. We will gladly sign it and include a personalization to fit the occasion and recipient.